MLA Index and Bibliography Series
Linda I. Solow, Editor

18th-Century American Secular Music Manuscripts: An Inventory

by
James J. Fuld
and
Mary Wallace Davidson

Philadelphia
Music Library Association, Inc.

MLA Index and Bibliography Series Number 20

International Standard Book Number: 0-914954-16-4
Library of Congress Catalog Card Number: 79-92993

CONTENTS

Preface *vii*

Abbreviations *xiii*

PREFACE

Oscar Sonneck has ably recorded 18th-century American printed music in his *A Bibliography of Early Secular American Music*, and his work has been amplified by William T. Upton.[1] There has not however been a companion census of 18th-century American secular music manuscripts, and it is our purpose here to present such a survey, documenting the popularity of the printed editions as well as of the music apparently not published in America during these years.

On the basis of a large random sampling, more than seventy-five percent of the titles indexed below are in neither Sonneck-Upton nor Wolfe.[2] Some of these are indeed foreign in origin, as are many of those in Sonneck-Upton and Wolfe. Many were evidently copied from British editions cited in *The British Union-Catalogue of Early Music Printed before the Year 1801*[3] (hereafter BUC). Some were known principally after 1800, but are included here because of their appearance in manuscripts with earlier works.

It is difficult to determine the date of music manuscript collections. The date of 18th-century printed music can usually be fixed or reasonably estimated, if not from a date on its title-page, from its imprint, copyright notice, or a contemporary advertisement. A manuscript collection, on the other hand, usually lacks a title-page or date, and is frequently compiled over a period of years by one or more persons. Moreover the presence of a date in a copybook may mean a commencement, conclusion, or presentation date. We have therefore tried to limit our census to manuscripts we believe to have been started prior to 1801, but which may also continue into a later repertory. In only one instance (MS No. 55) did clear

----

1. Sonneck's work was first published by the Library of Congress in Washington in 1905. The revised and enlarged edition by William Treat Upton (hereafter Sonneck-Upton) was similarly published in 1945, and reprinted in 1964 by Da Capo Press, New York. A few American manuscripts were recorded by Sonneck, and more were added by Upton.

2. Richard J. Wolfe's *Secular Music in America 1801-1825* (New York: The New York Public Library, 1964; hereafter, Wolfe) included further information on pre-1801 printed music in Appendices I-III.

3. London: Butterworths Scientific Publications, 1957.

internal distinctions enable us to exclude these later compositions from the inventory.

Only manuscripts which contain music are described; thus, collections which include only song-texts (i.e., "songsters") are omitted,[4] as are the collections consisting entirely of hymns or other religious pieces.[5] Only manuscripts which seem to have been written in America are included. A few manuscripts that do not meet the above criteria have nevertheless been included and briefly described for reasons noted in the individual entries.

Some of the manuscripts in the Moravian Music Foundation at Winston Salem, North Carolina, have been described with musical incipits by Marilyn Gombosi in her *Catalog of the Johannes Herbst Collection*.[6] All of the Winston Salem manuscripts as well as those of the Moravian Archives at Bethlehem, Pennsylvania, have been described with musical incipits in a recently completed unpublished catalog available at both locations. For this reason, as well as the special character of this repertory, we have excluded these manuscripts from our inventory. We have also omitted three manuscripts of keyboard music copied by Francis Hopkinson located at the Van Pelt Library of the University of Pennsylvania, because of their chiefly European repertory.

Also excluded are a large number of manuscripts located concurrently by Kate Van Winkle Keller. A thematic inventory of her findings (including MSS Nos. 2, 4-6, 11, 13, 21-22, 37, 45, and 47 below) is included in the National Tune Index, a data base being compiled by Keller and Carolyn Rabson. The contents of this data base will be published in microfiche by University Music Editions, and a checklist of all manuscripts will be published by the Music Library Association. A bibliography of dance manuscripts, compiled by Keller and Joy Van Cleef, will appear separately.[7]

The present publication then is a bibliographical study, with index, which describes in detail about half the presently located secular manuscripts as examples of musical and social history, documenting what music was

4. Printed collections are now well documented in Irving Lowens' *Bibliography of Songsters Printed in America before 1821* (Worcester, Mass.: American Antiquarian Society, 1976).

5. Printed collections will be described in detail in *Sacred Music in America through 1810*, a bibliography by Allen P. Britton, Irving Lowens and Richard Crawford, tentatively scheduled for publication in 1979.

6. Chapel Hill: University of North Carolina Press, 1970; a microfiche edition of the collection was published by University Music Editions in 1978.

7. In "The Dance and Its Music in Early New England," in *Early Music in Massachusetts* (Boston, The Colonial Society of Massachusetts, forthcoming).

popularly performed by both amateurs and "professionals" in an age when printed editions were expensive and scarce. The index provides the clues to what general types as well as specific titles were most and least common, while the bibliographic description serves to provide the context of their use.

Included are eighty-five secular musical manuscripts held by twenty libraries and private individuals. The manuscripts vary from one musical piece to collections of about four hundred pieces, and include a variety of types: keyboard sonatas, suites, variations, and other classical forms, military marches and bugle calls, ballroom dances, ballads, children's songs, folk songs, and theater music.

The manuscripts have been charming to examine. The personality of the compiler is evident from the selection and arrangement of pieces, the spelling mistakes, the occasional musical comments, the sentimental dedications, the precision or imprecision of the writing for emphasis, and the unanticipated crowdings at the ends of pages. These individual characteristics, coupled with the patina of old paper, faded ink, old style spellings and old bindings, add an almost human quality to a bibliographic inquiry.

Findings interesting to the compiler are:

(a) The earliest known American secular music manuscripts preceded the earliest known American printed editions by some years.

(b) Manuscripts were often copied from published works. See especially MS No. 85, pp. 38-39, in which the published source is clearly cited in the entry.

(c) The manuscript collections of at least two fifers during the Revolutionary War are known (MSS No. 1 and 45).

(d) The most frequently included title was "Washington's March," which appeared 20 times in 15 manuscripts. The title, "President's March," appeared in 17 manuscripts. There are several musical variants of both titles.

(e) The melody of "Yankee Doodle" appeared in 16 manuscripts, but never with text. One song-text does appear in a manuscript of poems bearing a date of 1779 (MS No. 44), but without the melody.

(f) We already know that the melody later used for "The Star Spangled Banner" appeared in several printed American music collections before 1800. "Anacreon in Heaven," the original British text to this melody, appeared in one manuscript, and "Adams and Liberty," a 1798 American text to the melody, appeared in eight manuscripts.

(g) The manuscripts of some honored American musical personalities have survived: Benjamin Carr (MSS No. 7-8, 34-36, 57, and 65), James Hewitt (No. 68), Francis Hopkinson (Nos. 9 and 33), and Alexander Reinagle (Nos. 12, 69-72, and perhaps 59). Some of these are autographs.

(h) Some melodies, chiefly European, popular in America before 1800 are still familiar today:

Adeste Fideles (or Portuguese Hymn)
Anacreon in Heaven or Adams and Liberty (melody of
   The Star Spangled Banner)
The British Grenadiers
The Campbells are Coming (known in the 18th century
   as Hob Nob)
God Save the King
Green Sleeves
Irish Wash[er]woman
Malbrouk (melody of For He's a Jolly Good Fellow)
Marseillaise
Molly Put the Kettle On
O Dear What Can the Matter Be
Rule Britannia
The Sailor's Hornpipe (or The College Hornpipe)
Yankee Doodle

   This survey of 18th-century American secular music
manuscripts was initially planned by James J. Fuld as an
article for Music Library Association *Notes*, but quickly
became longer than space permitted. It consisted of an
introduction, a description of each manuscript with a simple
listing, and index of titles. When the Music Library
Association determined to publish the survey in book form,
it also decided to include a more detailed description of
each manuscript, and an index (and therefore citation) of
first lines, as well as names and subjects. Mary Davidson
kindly undertook these extensive revisions, as well as
completely editing the work, resulting in a significant
increase in the amount of information contained in the
survey.

   All the libraries and private collectors represented
in the studies by Sonneck-Upton or Wolfe, as well as others,
participated in this census. Appreciation is expressed to
the music librarians, manuscript librarians, and rare book
librarians, and to the private collectors for their cooper-
ation in making this study possible. Especial thanks are
due to Kate Van Winkle Keller for the enthusiastic alacrity
with which she shared the fruits of her research, as well
as her continued advice and criticism; to Bruce Gustafson
and David Young for examining the manuscripts in Michigan
and Chicago respectively; to Shirley Piper Emanuel for her
help in the initial stages of revision and to Michal
Truelsen for hers in the final throes; and to Irving and
Margery Lowens for their generosity of spirit and deed.

                *   *   *

Since it was impossible in most cases to determine
reliably either the compiler, the date, or the intended
medium of performance, the manuscripts have been arranged
alphabetically by state, and further subdivided by city
and library.

Each manuscript description begins with a heading
showing its current location (state, city, institution or
person, library, and shelf number if any). Then follows
the bibliographic citation of the manuscript giving the
descriptive or actual title, pagination, and size. In the
descriptive title the term "commonplace book" indicates a
small book not usually intended for music, often containing
poems, accounts, and jottings of various sorts. "Copybook"
indicates a volume in which staff lines were often hand-
ruled throughout in advance. Notes describe (in order):
binding, hand(s), ink, paper, inscribed names and/or dates,
miscellaneous notes, and, in general, the music. Provenance
in most cases was not readily obtainable, and so omitted.

Where sacred works occur as a section of the manuscript,
they are described and indexed by genre, but not cited
individually. Where they occur interspersed among the
secular works, they are cited and indexed by title and/or
first line as well. The same is true for songs in languages
other than English.

Printed sources for titles have not been cited. Many
are recorded in BUC, Sonneck-Upton or Wolfe, as well as in
the forthcoming *National Tune Index* by Keller and Rabson.[8]

Original spellings of titles, first lines, and attributions have been retained in the entries and resolved in the
indices only when conflicting forms resulted in too wide a
separation between initial words, even though we were
reluctant to force congruity in the absence of thematic
indices. Since most spelling is phonetic, however, it is
doubtful that such evidence may be used to prove the source
from which the compiler copied.

In the inventories a title cited alone indicated the
appearance of a melody without words, on a single stave
(unless otherwise noted in the descriptive paragraphs above
the entry). Presence of an accompanying song-text is
shown by citation of the first line, indented on the line
below; such a text is assumed to be underlain unless otherwise noted, and the format of succeeding verses, if any,
is indicated in a note at a further indention (e.g., "vv.
2-3 underlaid," or "vv.2-3 as text"). The number and
character of vocal or instrumental parts are also indicated
in the note position if not already indicated in, or if
different from, the general notes in the paragraphs
describing the manuscript as a whole. For example, in
MS No. 4, the following entry

          6   Sheep in thy clusters
                      Her sheep had in clusters
                         3 parts (2 treble and bass); vv. 2-3 as text

indicates that beginning on page 6 will be found a song with

8. To be published by University Music Editions, New
York City.

text entitled (by the MS compiler) "Sheep in Thy Clusters;"
the first line of text begins, "Her sheep had in clusters,"
and the first verse is copied throughout the melody while
verses two and three appear in poetic format; there are two
treble parts and a bass line which may have been intended
for a vocal trio, a vocal duet, or vocal solo, with or
without accompaniment, or for keyboard alone.

ABBREVIATIONS

BUC - *The British Union-Catalogue of Early Music Printed before the Year 1801* (London: Butterworths Scientific Publications, 1957).

MS(S) - manuscript(s)

p(p) - page(s)

Sonneck-Upton - Sonneck, Oscar G. T., and Upton, William Treat, *A Bibliography of Early Secular American Music* (Washington, 1945; reprinted New York: Da Capo, 1964)

v(v) - verse(s)

Wolfe - Wolfe, Richard J., *Secular Music in America 1801-1825* (New York: The New York Public Library, 1964)

INVENTORY

1. *CONNECTICUT: NEW HAVEN. YALE UNIVERSITY, MUSIC LIBRARY. Ma12.094.*

"A MOST EXCELLENT AND ELEGANT COLLECTION OF AIRS, MARCHES, MINUETTS, DUETTS, &c., &c., SET AND ADOPTED FOR TWO VIOLINS, OR OTHER INSTRIMENTS. SELECTED FROM THE BEST WORKS OF THE MOST ADMIRED AUTHERS BOTH ANCIENT AND MODERN. BY JOHN F. CURTISS [NAME CROSSED THROUGH], MUSICIAN. $2.00." 1/2 leaf, t.p., [166] pp. 13 x 21.5 cm.

Cover title: "Lauren Hotchkiss Book."

Bound in brown half-leather and marbled paper over boards.

Entries in same hand and on same kind of paper but in different inks.

Inscriptions: "John F. Curtiss [name crossed through] booke" and below, "Lauren Hotch-kiss's Property," and in different ink, "Bela E. Hotchkiss," inside front cover; maxims by Shakespeare and Garrick, and "Lauren Hotch-kiss's Property, price $2.00," on following leaf, torn off at bottom.

Vignette: lute, flute, and another woodwind instrument (with bell) behind open music book bearing legend, "Let him who hates music be kept at least three paces distant," in water-color, inside front cover.

According to a note in the hand of E. J. O'Meara, Curtiss was made a freeman in Cheshire, Connecticut, in 1803. He is named as composer of the following titles: Jefferson's March, Warren's March, March in A Midnight Serenade, Duetto, Amelia, Rondo, March of the Disbanded Troops.

Music on 2 staves in treble clefs, without words. Contains some written-out ornamentation.

Page [Pagination supplied]

1 Lesson 1. God Save the King
       2. Madam Plaud's
              Allemand
       3. Felton's Gavot

2 Gavot by Felton
   Handel's Claronett

3 Minuett by Vanhall

4 Merseilles Hymn

Page [Pagination supplied]

5 Sir Sidney Smith's Minuett
   Portegues Hymn

6 Duett No. I. Andante amoroso

7 Duett No. II. Allegro. Celebrated
       Air in *The Haunted Tower*
       [by] Pleyel.

8 Duett No. III. Celebrated move-
       ment of Heydn

1. CONNECTICUT: NEW HAVEN. YALE UNIVERSITY (JOHN F. CURTISS)

2. *CONNECTICUT: NEW HAVEN. YALE UNIVERSITY, STERLING MEMORIAL LIBRARY, MANUSCRIPTS AND ARCHIVES. MISC. MSS. 72; MICROFILM 44.*

COMMONPLACE BOOK OF MUSIC COMPILED BY AARON THOMPSON.
127 pp. 15.5 x 21 cm.

> Bound in half-leather (deteriorated) over boards. Pagination added in later hand, in pencil, over original item numbers; lacking pp. 13-14.

> All entries in same hand except p. 54, by Caleb Jeffries; same ink and paper.

Inscriptions:

> Names: Aaron Thompson, pp. 23, 30, 32, 37, 39 and "Aaron Thompson practist these tunes on the first day of April in the year one thousand seven hundred and eighty," pp. 42, 43 (twice), 44, 46, 48; Chloe Thompson, p.32; David Rogers, p.40; Caleb Jeffries, "bought from Alette, widow of Aaron Thompson [certification of purchase]," p.54.

> Dates: 1777, p.46; 1779, p.34; 1780, pp.38,45;

1782, p. 48.

Aaron Thompson was a fifer in the 3rd New Jersey Regiment under Col. Elias Dayton; MS also contains miscellaneous accounts, exercises, and notes regarding the regiment's activities, 1777-1782.

A Table of Time, p.3. Partial index, pp. 5-8, completed by inserted leaves of a much later hand.

Figures for country dances inscribed for the following titles: "Sweet Richard" and "Miss More's Rant," p. 49; "Flowers of Edenburough," p. 50; "The Dutchess of Brumswick Country Dance," p. 51; "Allmon Swiss Country Dance," p. 52.

Melody only, without words. Music, pp. 9-58 only.

Page

9 Damon & Phyllis. A Troop
   The Drummer's Call
   The King of Prussia's
     March of Hunting
     For bass line, see p. 26
     below.

10 Captain Clark's Quickstep
   Prety Cubit [i.e., Pretty
     Cupid]. A Retreat

11 St. Patrick's Day in the
     Morning
   Salle Kelle O'. A Quick Step

12 Capt. Gordan's Quick Step
     of the 36th
   The English Fuzeleers
     March. A Quickstep
   The Three Camps. A Reveilly

*13 The Hessian Reveilly
   The Scots Reveilly
   The Read Joke

*14 The Temple[?]. A Troop
   Lady Hope's Reel
   Capt. Read's March

15 Farewell to Elizabeth
     Town. A Quick [Step]
   The Duke's March

Page

   Lovly Nancy. A Retreat

16 Young Jack. A Qick [sic] Step
   Lady Washington Quick Step
   Nomber Three. A Quick Step

17 Now I Am Willing. A Quick Step
   Lady Coventry's Minuet

18 The Granadiers March
   The Marquis of Granby's or 7th
     Troop of Hon. Ganediers
     March

19 This Day We Sail. A Quick Step
   The White Cockade. A Quick Step
   To Arms

20 The Boy in the Basket. A Quick
     [Step]
   The Basket of Oysters. A Quick
     Step
   The Pineers' March

21 The Roast Beef of Old England
   Whoza for France & Spain

22 Number One. A Quick Step
   A Quick Step
   The Generl

23 A Brandy & Wine. A Quick Step

—————————

*These pages now missing; titles supplied from index.

2. CONNECTICUT: NEW HAVEN. YALE UNIVERSITY (AARON THOMPSON)

3. *DISTRICT OF COLUMBIA: WASHINGTON.   LIBRARY OF CONGRESS, MUSIC DIVISION. M63.A2M8 CASE.*

"WILLIAM O. ADAMS'S MUSIC BOOK, LONDON, SEPTEMBER 4TH, 1795." 44 pp. 14 x 22 cm.

Bound in paper over boards. Lacking pp. 5-6; pp. 35 and 41 omitted in pagination.

Entries in same primitive hand and ink (a few in pencil) and on same paper.

Inscription: place and date repeated on rear cover.

For treble melody instrument (flute, fife, or violin), unless otherwise noted.

Page
1   Jemmys Return
    Who'll Buy Prim Roses

2   For [i.e., Poor] Jack -
        Primo

3   Oh My Bonny Bet - Primo
    La belle Catherine
    Capt. MacKintosh's Fancy

4   Rhode Island March
    The New Pump Room
    The Bouquet
    Never 'till Now, I Felt
        Love's Smart

7   The Good Girl - a Country
        Dance
    All My Past Life &c

8   The Marchioness
    Return Enraptured Hours

9   The Mulberry Tree
    Fresh & Strong
    Fisher's Minuett

10 Bright Phoebus - Primo

11 My Daddy Oh Was Very
        Good - in *The Farmer*
    Bow Wow Wow

12 Charming Village Maid -
        in *The Farmer*
    The Madrigal

13 The Rose Tree
    The Way Worn Traveller -
        in *The Mounteneers*
    Swiss Guards March

Page
14 Heaving of the Lead - Primo
    Marionets Cottillion

15 The Hayden
    The God of Love
    Yankee Doodle

16 The Ploughman Turned Sailor

17 The Greenwich Prisoner, by Dibdin
    Henry's Cottage Maid
    Oxford Road to Pantheon

18 Jove in His Chair, in the
        Burletta of *Midas*
    Pauvre Madelon - Duett in *The
        Surrender of Calais*
        Primo only.

19 Fisher's Hornpipe - *Rosina*
    Ricketts Hornpipe

20 Trio in *Rosina*: When the Rosy
        Morn Appearing
        For 3 flutes.
    Song in *Rosina*: The Morn Returns

21 When William at Eve - Song
        in *Rosina*
    I Lock'd up All My Treasure -
        Quaker

22 Placide's Cotillion
    The Ball

23 Oh Dear What Can the Matter Be
    Heathen Mythology
    The Cornplanter - a Country
        Dance
    Columbia - a New Country Dance
        Followed by dance figures.

3. *DISTRICT OF COLUMBIA: WASHINGTON. LIBRARY OF CONGRESS (WILLIAM O. ADAMS)*

Page

24 Blodget's Minuett
Chorus Jigg
Hay Makers' Dance
Fandango

25 Hessian Guards March
Apollo – a Country Dance
The Marquiss de La
Fayette's March

26 Massachusetts March, by
Granger

27 And Did You Not Hear of a
Jolly Young Waterman
Old Woman Tost in a Blanket

28 Hymn de Marseillois

29 The Duke of York's March
Constansy

30 Turks March
The Poor Soldier

31 The Topsail Shivers in
the Wind
The Little Devil Dance

32 Finale to the Opera of *Rosina*

33 Desponding Negro
Philadelphia Fusileers March

Page

34 Minuet by Belstead

36 Since Kathlean Has Proved So
Untrue, in *The Poor Soldier*
La lumiere, a Favourite French
Song

37 Heave the Anchor Short
How Imperfect Is Expression

38 The Golden Days, of Good
Queen Bess
Drink to Me Only

39 Sung by Mrs. Smith, in
The Deserter

40 Je suis Lindor, chanson francois

42 Mary's Dream

43 The Streamlet
On an overlay.

44 The Presidents March – Primo
The tune is not inscribed;
instead is a pencilled
tune, The Tank, followed
by Mary's Tears (title
only).

4. *DISTRICT OF COLUMBIA: WASHINGTON. LIBRARY OF CONGRESS, MUSIC DIVISION. M1.A1A CASE.*

COPYBOOK OF MUSIC COMPILED BY THE REV. WILKES ALLEN,
PROBABLY IN 1790.   146 [i.e., 150] pp.   19 x 30 cm.

Original cover title: *Apollo* (determined from
Library's catalog card).

20th-century library binding in green half-leather
with marbled paper over boards; overlay from
original copybook pasted inside front cover.
Lacking pp. 48-49 and 52-53; p. 67 omitted in
pagination; beginning at p. 143 only rectos
of leaves are numbered.

Entries in same hand and ink; many different
papers revealed by a variety of watermarks.

Inscriptions: "Mr. Allen's," inside front cover;
"The notes in this Book of Songs were transcribed
by Rev. Wilkes Allen during his apprenticeship
at the carpentering business, in 1790. Several
pieces are original: 'The Butterfly,' page 14;
'The Sleeping Daughter,' page 31; 'The Rose,'
page 50; 'The Reply,' page 79; 'The Cricket,'
page 81," and "Presented to Wilkes Allen, D.D.S.
by his mother, Mrs. Mary Allen, 1846," p. [1];
"April 28 1801," p. [144*v*].

Explanation of musical terms, p. 142.

Songs, hymns, and part-songs (chiefly duets),
notated for treble and bass (i.e., with keyboard accompaniment), unless otherwise indicated.

Page

<table>
<tr><td>2</td><td>The Quick March
3 parts (2 treble and
bass).</td></tr>
<tr><td></td><td>The sun sets at night and
the stars shun the day
Vv. 1-3 as text.</td></tr>
<tr><td>3</td><td>The Soldier, Sung by an
Officer before the
Taking of Quebeck
How stands the glass around
Vv. 1-3 as text.</td></tr>
<tr><td>13</td><td>The Traveler, set by B. Brown
The traveler benighted
Vv. 1-3 as text.</td></tr>
<tr><td>5</td><td>The Wanderer
Ceas[e] a while ye winds
to blow
Vv. 1-3 as text.</td></tr>
<tr><td>14</td><td>The Butterfly, set by W. Allen,
written on the occasion of
a young lady's putting a
butterfly out at the
window who had spent the
winter in her chamber
Go happy insect flit thy way
Vv. 1-3 as text.</td></tr>
<tr><td>6</td><td>Sheep in thy Clusters
Her sheep had in clusters
3 parts (2 treble and
bass); vv. 2-3 as text.</td></tr>
<tr><td>15</td><td>Winter
When winter robes the hills
& plains
Vv. 1-3 as text.</td></tr>
<tr><td>8</td><td>The Masons Daughter
3 parts (2 treble
and bass).</td></tr>
<tr><td>16</td><td>Guardian Angels
Guardian angels now protect me
Vv. 1-8 as text.</td></tr>
<tr><td>9</td><td>The Red House
I will my humors</td></tr>
<tr><td>17</td><td>Are You Sure the News Is True
Are you sure the news is true
3 parts (primo, secundo,
and baso); vv. 1-2 as text
following the next title.
Washington's March</td></tr>
<tr><td>10</td><td>Cotillion</td></tr>
<tr><td>11</td><td>Silvander
Apollo
Ah dear mama shall I tell
Baltimore
Words only.</td></tr>
<tr><td>18</td><td>Chain Cotillion
Boston's March</td></tr>
<tr><td>12</td><td>The Indian Warrior</td></tr>
</table>

(11)

4. *DISTRICT OF COLUMBIA: WASHINGTON. LIBRARY OF CONGRESS (WILKES ALLEN)*

Page

I once was a saylor
Vv. 1-6 as text.

55 Wallsall. P. M.
Ye servants of God your
master proclaim
3 parts (2 treble and
bass); vv. 2-5 as text.

57 [Blank]

58 [Blank]

59 Damon to Delia. Words by
Majr. Andre
Ah! Delia see the fatal
hour
3 parts (2 treble and
bass); vv. 1-4, 6
as text.

61 Young Johnny the Miller
Young Johnny the miller
Bass only; words as
text (verses indis-
tinguishable).

63 Vicar of Bray
Of Bray the vicar
Melody only (incomplete);
vv. 1-3 as text.

65 Mary's Dream
The moon has climbed
the highest hill

68 The Black Sloven
As I was a walking
1 v. as text.

70 Soldiers Farewell, by Swan
At leangth too soon
dear creature
1 v. as text.

71 [Blank]

72 Hook & Crook. B. Brown
A few years ago in the
days of my granum
Vv. 1-3 as text.

74 [Blank]

75 The Miller

Page

Though eyes may speak pleasure
Vv. 1-3 as text.

76 Strephen & Delia
Bright Sol at length by
theater woods
Vv. 1-6 as text.

77 Indian Chief
Words only.

78 The Jolly Miller
Thus like the miller
bold & free
Vv. 1-4 as text.

79 The Reply. Wilkes Allen
By the side of a stream
Vv. 1-3 as text.

80 [Blank]

81 Cricket. Words by Cowper. Set
by W. Allen.
Little inmate full of mirth
Vv. 1-3 as text.

82 Handell's Waterpiece
2 treble parts.

83 Handell's Clarinet
3 parts (2 treble and
bass).

84 Elmira. W. Allen
Ye swains and gentle virgins
come
3 parts (2 treble and
bass); vv. 1-3 as text.

86 Belisle's March
A term full as long as the
siege of old Troy
2 treble parts; vv. 1-5
as text.

87 The Pigeon
Why taries my love
Vv. 1-5 as text.

88 The Shepherds Complaint
Oh nightingale best poet
of the grove
Vv. 1-4 as text.

4. *DISTRICT OF COLUMBIA: WASHINGTON. LIBRARY OF CONGRESS (WILKES ALLEN)*

Page

89 Highland Queen, [by] Swan
No more my song shall be
my swains
Vv. 1-4 as text.

90 Andre
Return enraptured hour
Melody only; vv. 1-4
as text.

91 A Gipsy Ballad, set by
B. Brown
A wandring gipsy sirs, I am
Vv. 1-5 as text.

92 Irish Lamentation
When I lived with my
granmam
Vv. 1-3 as text.

93 The Year, [by] Brown
Just as the year is,
so the span
Vv. 1-3 as text.

94 Lass of Richmond Hill
On Richmond hill there
lived a lass
Vv. 1-3 as text.

95 Bonny Bett
No more I'll court the
town bred fair
Vv. 1-4 as text.

96 The Fragrant Lily
The fragrant lily of
the vale
Vv. 1-4 as text.

97 Lady Washington
I saw you my hero
Vv. 1-4 as text.

99 Bright Phoebus
Bright Phoebus has
mounted the chariot
of day
Vv. 1-3 as text.

101 Orne's March
3 parts (2 treble and
bass).

Page

102 Cynthia
Rise Cynthia rise
3 parts (2 treble and bass).

103 God of Love
3 parts (2 treble and in-
complete bass). See also
p. 108 below.

104 Crazy Jane
Why fair maid in every
feature
1 v. as text.

106 The Gally Slave
Oh! think on my fate
Vv. 1-3 as text.

108 Ma chère amie
Melody only.
God of Love
3 parts (2 treble and bass).
See also p. 103 above.

109 Washington's March
3 parts (2 treble and bass).

111 [Blank]

112 Extracted from Handels *Messiah*
How beautiful are the feet
3 parts (2 treble and bass).

114 Extract from Handel's *Messiah*
He shall feed his flock
5 parts (4 treble and bass).

119 Blackbird

120 Massachusetts March
3 parts (2 treble and bass).

121 Presidents March

122 Duke of York's March
3 parts (2 treble and bass).

124 Cap'n Makintosh's
Melody only.

125 Miller's Air
Melody only.

126 [Blank]

127 Minuet. Handel
3 parts (2 treble and bass).

Page

128 Capt. Brown's March
    3 parts (2 treble and
    bass).

130 The Sweet Little Girl That
    I Love
    My friends all declare
    V. 2 as text.

131 [Blank]

132 Friend & Pitcher
    My friend so rare
    Melody only; vv.
    1-2 as text.

133 The All of Life
    When first the humble roof
    I knew
    Vv. 1-2 as text.

134-37 [Blank]

138 A View of Death
    Ah! Lovely appearance
    of Death
    V. 1 repeated as text,
    with vv. 2-9.

140 Jove in His Chair
    3 parts (2 treble and
    bass).

Page

141 Hymne de Marseillois

143 [Blank]

[143*v*] Untitled]
    When Anna seated on a
    ____[illegible]
    Words only.

144 [Blank]

[144*v*] Arabella
    Say have you seen my
    Arabella
    Words only.

145 [Blank]

[145*v*] The Silver Moon
    Where where where shall I
    seek the lovely swain
    Words only.

146 [Blank]

[146*v*] Dear Nancy
    I've sailed the world
    all around
    Melody only; vv. 1-3
    as text.

5. *DISTRICT OF CLOUMBIA: WASHINGTON.   LIBRARY OF CONGRESS, MUSIC DIV-
ISION.   M63.B4 CASE.*

COPYBOOK CONTAINING FLUTE MUSIC, COMPILED BY HENRY
BECK, 1786.   23, 158, [19] pp. 17.5 x 21.5 cm.

Bound in leather. Lacking beginning pp. 1-3.

Entries in same hand and ink and on same paper.

Inscription: "Copied by Henry Beck in the year
1786," on front fly-leaf.

The instructions for flute in the beginning
are identical to those in both *The Compleat
Tutor for the German Flute* ([1775]) and *Compleat
Instruction for the German Flute* ([178-?]).

5. DISTRICT OF COLUMBIA: WASHINGTON. LIBRARY OF CONGRESS (HENRY BECK)

6. *DISTRICT OF COLUMBIA: WASHINGTON. LIBRARY OF CONGRESS (BELLAMY BAND BOOK)*

Page

Page		Page	
143	The Happy Bacchanalain Britannia's Invitation	151	Hero and Leander Behind the Bush Susan's Favourite
144	Colin and Phyllis Castle Berry	152	When I Follow'd a Lass, in *Love in a Village* The Triumph of Bacchus
145	The Bottle The Court of Vauxhall	153	Fain Would I Have Her General Wolfe
146	How Stands the Glass Around 2 treble parts. Here's to the Maiden of Bashful Fifteen	154	The President's March 2 treble parts.
147	Polly The English Padlock	155	Birks of Endermay
148	The Dusky Night Happy Hours	156	[Untitled march]
149	The Masquerade Minuet 2 treble parts.	157	Philadelphia March
150	Why Heaves My Fond Bosom Ye Nymphs and Swains	158	[Untitled minuet]

Following Page

[1-19 Blank]

6. *DISTRICT OF COLUMBIA: WASHINGTON. LIBRARY OF CONGRESS, MUSIC DIVISION. M1200.B45 CASE.*

"THE PROPERTY OF BELLAMY BAND, JUNE 1799." 82 pp. 13 x 20 cm.

Binding in very poor condition.

Entries in different hands and inks but on same paper.

Inscription: Title as above, on engraved ornamental title-page, bearing printed legend, "Sold by Cahusac & Sons, 196 Strand, London."

Entries on pp. 1-43 are for 3 parts (2 treble and bass), and those on pp. 44-67 are for treble melody only, unless otherwise indicated; pp. 68-82, containing only sacred works, have not been inventoried.

Page		Page	
1	Banks of the Swale	6	40th Regiment
2	General Burgoynes March	7	The Democrat
4	Washington's March	8	How Imperfect Is Expression

Page

Page

10	Maul Brook
11	Yankee Doodle
12	York Fusaleer
14	Presidents March
16	Coldstreams
18	Feltons Air
19	Row Dow Dow
20	Colo. Bellamys March
22	General Greens March
23	Clarionet March
24	Truxton Forever
25	Ive's Air
26	Dauphin
27	Freemasons March
28	[Untitled march]
30	[Untitled]
	Middle voice incomplete.
31	God Save the King
32	[Untitled march]
34	Harisons Compound March
35	March in *Bluebeard*
36	Colo. Balls Marche
39	[Untitled march]
41	Jeffersons Liberty
42	[Untitled march]
44	Lovely Nance
45	17th Regiment
	Freemasons Farewell
	The Rose Tree
46	Barbadoes
	Federal March
47	The Exile of Erin
	Roslin Castle
48	Washington's Grand March

	The Oak
	The Trooper
49	O Dear What Can the Matter Be
	New Haven March
	Yanke Doode
50	Rogues March
	Buonaparte's Grand March
51	An Elegy on the Death of
	Genl Washington
	Successful Campaign
	Paddy Whake
52	The Death March
	The Owen
	The Faithful Lover
	Alas my heart, alas my
	heart
	Ye Greenfields
53	St. Patricks Day
	Love Forever
	Lochaber
54	The Heavenly Vision
	I beheld and to a great
	multitude
	Bass only.
55	Mary's Dream
	The moon had climbed the
	highest hill
	Blue Bell of Scotland
56	Newburgh
	Let evry creature join
	Bass and textual incipit
	only.
57	Jerusalem LM Psalm 17
	Bass only.
58	New York
	Bass only.
60	Confession LM
	2 parts (treble and
	bass).
62	Serenade
	Fresh or Strong
	Coronation
	All hail the power of Jesus
	name

7.   DISTRICT OF COLUMBIA: WASHINGTON.   LIBRARY OF CONGRESS (BENJAMIN CARR DUETS)

Page

      The Young Widow

63 Funeral dirge
      Farewell, farewell a sad
      long farewell

64 Christmas Ode
      At this unwanted hour
      Bass only.

Page

65 Alpha
      When faith presents the
      Saviors death

66 Chesterfield LM
      Bass only.

67 Mary's Dream
      The moon had climb'd
      the hiest hill

7.   DISTRICT OF COLUMBIA: WASHINGTON.   LIBRARY OF CONGRESS, MUSIC DIVISION.   ML96.C28 CASE.

COPYBOOK CONTAINING VOCAL DUETS.   [20] pp.
30 x 24 cm.

Unbound; appears to have been previously enclosed in binding.   Upper part of p. [5] cut away.

Entries on pp. [5]-[11] are known to be in the hand of Benjamin Carr.

Inscription: Initials "B C" inscribed after title, p. [5], perhaps indicating that Carr was the composer of at least this melody. None of the melodies in his hand are the presently familiar tunes.

For 2 treble voices and unfigured bass; includes one solo song with bass (No. 3); interlinear words.

Page [Pagination supplied]

1 Unless with Amanda, a Favorite Canzonet by Storace
    Being a "title-page" only for the following:

2 Canzonet by Storace
    Unless with my Amanda blest

4 [Blank]

5 No. 1. Giddy Gout
    Giddy giddy gout your shirt hangs out

Page [Pagination supplied]

6 No. 2. Ride a Cock Horse
    Ride a cock horse to Banbury cross

7 No. 3. Little Robin Red Breast
    Little Robin Red Breast sit upon a rail

8 No. 4. Pat a Cake
    Pat a cake, pat a cake
    Open score.
    No. 5. Baa Lamb
    Baa lamb, baa lamb

Page [Pagination supplied]   Page [Pagination supplied]

9   No. 6. Multiplication
        Multiplication, vexation

10   No. 7. Hey Diddle Diddle
        Hey diddle diddle

12   [Blank]

13   Duetto tutto da voi dipende
        del Sigr Paisello nella
        Locandiera [i.e., *La*
        Locanda]
        Tutto da voi dipende

8.   *DISTRICT OF COLUMBIA: WASHINGTON. LIBRARY OF CONGRESS, MUSIC DIV-*
    ISION. ML96.C28 CASE.

"CARR, [BENJAMIN.] MANUSCRIPT COLLECTION OF
PIANOFORTE MUSIC."   82 pp.   28 x 23 cm.

Title from label on binder's case; original
binding in half-leather over boards.

All entries except the first (pp. 2-8) are
known to be in the hand of Benjamin Carr; pages
and leaves numbered in a later hand; different
papers.

Inscription: "B. Carr," upper right corner, p. 1,
and after title, p. 8.

For keyboard (harpsichord or pianoforte); one
entry (pp. 37-61) specifically for 2 harpsichords;
the work by Edelmann (pp. 27-35) published in
London (1785) "for harpsichord or piano forte,
with an accompanyment for a violin."

Page   Page

1   [Blank]

2   Overture de *Semele* del Sigr
       G. F. Handel

8   Menuett

9   8th Concerto Correlli No. 8
       Vivace, p. 9, incomplete.

19   Paradies

23   [Blank]

24   Giga

26   [Blank]

27   Sonata 1 Op 7 Edelmann
       Caption title, p. 28:
       La capricieuse.

36   [Blank]

37   Duett for Two Harpsichord[s]
       Open score: treble, bass,
       and bass clefs.

62   Sonata [?]
       By D. Scarlatti,
       according to cataloger's
       note.

64   [Blank]

67   Medley Overture
       Reduced score (orches-
       tration indicated).

81   [Blank]

82   [Blank]

9. *DISTRICT OF COLUMBIA: WASHINGTON. LIBRARY OF CONGRESS, MUSIC DIV-ISION. ML96.H83 CASE.*

"FRANCIS HOPKINSON HIS BOOK." [iv], 206 pp. 24 x 30 cm.

20th-century binding in half-leather and marble paper over boards; original book-plate, "Francis Hopkinson," pasted inside front cover. Lacking pp. 151-52 and 177-78.

Entries in same hand and ink and on same paper.

Inscriptions: "Philadelphia Domini 1759" in Hopkinson's hand, inside original front cover (according to an old typed catalog card, 1919); attributions to the compiler by initials "F. H." follow titles, pp. 63, 111, 163, 169, 179, and 180, the last dated 1760.

The MS is described in Sonneck-Upton, pp. 402-403. The song, "My Days Have Been So Wondrous Free (p. 63)," by Hopkinson, is believed to be the earliest extant secular composition by a native American composer, and is reproduced in facsimile in Sonneck's *Francis Hopkinson and James Lyon*, p. 31, and transcribed on p. 199. It is also reproduced in Sonneck's "Francis Hopkinson: The First American Poet-Composer and Our Musical Life in Colonial Times," vol. 3, p. 442.

Index, p. [iii].

Cantatas, songs, arias, or treble duets on 3 staves; keyboard accompaniment chiefly with figured bass; interlinear words.

Page		Page	
1	[Untitled] del. Signr. Palma Di render mi la calma	16	[Untitled] del. Signr. Vinci Per pieta bell idol mio
4	[Untitled] Alesandro dell' India Vinci Le mai turbo il tuo riposo Duet.	18	Aria francese Liapur Liapur d'amore
		19	Chetigiovaora Cheti gio vaora fille
8	[Untitled] del. Sign. Vinci Tu voi ch'io vivao cara Duet.	20	Bettina femo Bettina femo pace
		21	Mio cor Mio cor non ti lagniar
12	[Untitled] Vo sol cando un mar crudele	22	Ritorna al caro Ritorna al caro bene

Page

Page

Page

Page

169 [Untitled] F. H.
With pleasure have I
past my days
Vv. 2-6 as text.

170 Attic Fire
When all the attic fire
was fled

172 A Solemn Dirge in *Romeo and Juliet*
Rise, rise, rise, heart
breaking sighs
For solo with chorus
(SATB), the latter only
partially notated;
v. 2 as text.

174 Aminta
My sheep I neglected

175 The 4th Psalm
Oh Lord that art my
righteous judge
Duet.

176 Anthem
Thro' all the changing
scenes of life

179 The 23d Psalm. F. H.
The Lord himself, the
mighty Lord
Duet.

180 An Anthem from the 114th
Psalm. F. H. 1760.
What aileth thee
Duet.

182 Liberty, a Song in *Judas Machabeus*, by Mr. Handel
Tis liberty, dear liberty
alone

184 [Untitled] del Signr. Vinci
I doni non voglia
gl'affetti non curo
Duet.

187 Hymn
We adore and worship thee

188 Song in the Oratorio of *Samson*
My faith & truth
For solo voice and chorus;
parts not indicated.

190 Song in the Oratorio of *Samson*
Total eclipse. No sun. No
moon, all dark

191 Rondeau. Compos'd by Sigr.
D'Giardini
Voi amante che vedete

192 Song in the Oratorio *Samson*
Loud as the thunder's awful
voice
V. 2 as text.

195 Song in the Opera of *Semele*
Oh sleep, oh sleep why dost
thou leave me

196 Song in the Oratorio of *Samson*
Return, return O God
of hosts

198 O Let the Merry Bell Ring
Round
O let the merry bell
ring round

199 Hunting Song
The sun from ye east

200 Song
Let not rage

201 Song
Water parted from the sea

202 Song
If o'er the cruel tyrant

203 [Untitled]
In infancy our hopes & fears

204 [Untitled] By Dr. Purcell
Celebrate this festival

205 Song in *Judith*
Vain is beauty's gaudy
flow'r

10. *DISTRICT OF COLUMBIA: WASHINGTON. LIBRARY OF CONGRESS, MUSIC DIVISION. M1.A11 VOL. 26.*

SONGS BOUND AT END OF VOLUME OF MISCELLANEOUS PRINTED MUSIC.   175-217, [2] pp.   33 x 23 cm.

Bound in brown quarter-leather and marbled paper over boards; red leather label on cover bears gold-tooled name, "Eleanor P. Custis." Original page[s] lacking following p. 214.

Same hand except for last entry; same or similar ink and paper.   Pages numbered, and some attributions made, in pencil in later hand.

Inscriptions: "Maria Carter, 1799, Eleanor Parke Custis Lewis to Lawrence Lewis, 1798," recto of flyleaf; "Eleanor Parke Custis to Lawrence Lewis, 1799," and "Maria," verso of flyleaf; "1798," p. 198.

Eleanor Parke Custis, born March 21, 1779 in Abingdon, Va., was the granddaughter of Martha Custis.   She became the adopted daughter of George Washington and married his nephew, Lawrence Lewis, on February 22nd, 1799.   In the above inscriptions the combination of married name and date, recto of flyleaf, would therefore seem premature.   Concerning her musical training, particularly at the harpsichord, see Nicholas E. Tawa, "Secular Music in the Late Eighteenth-Century American Home."   See also Joseph Muller, *The Star Spangled Banner*, pp. 18-19 and 20, n. 5. Biographical reminiscences and portrait are found in George Washington Parke Custis, *Recollections and Private Memoirs of Washington by His Adopted Son*, especially pp. 40-45 and 408n.

The MS is described is described in *The Collector* 2(1890-91):61.

Songs with keyboard, in 2 staves unless otherwise noted; includes some works for voices and harp, or for keyboard alone.

Page

175   [Untitled]
    Amidst the illusions that
    oe'r the mind flutter
      Attributed to Shield,
      from *Hartford Bridge*
      [London, 1792].

179   [Blank]

Page

180   The Millers, a Sleep in
    His Mill
    My eyes may speak pleasure
    Vv. 2-3 as text; attributed
    to C. Dibdin, *Christmas
    Tale* [London, 1773].

11. *DISTRICT OF COLUMBIA: WASHINGTON. LIBRARY OF CONGRESS (EDWARD MURPHEY)*

Page

182 [Untitled]
    One day I heard Mary say
    For "harp" and "voce"
    with bass (3 staves);
    vv. 2-4 as text; attrib-
    ution: I'll Never Leave
    Thee - Scotch Air.

184 Arietta veneziana
    Quelle piu bianche
    For "harpa" and "voce"
    with bass (3 staves);
    v. 2 as text.

186 Pauvre Jacques
    Pauvre Jacques quand
    j'étais près de toi
    V. 2 as text; attributed
    to (or sung by)
    "Mme Travant."

188 Je pense à vous
    Je pense à vous where e'er
    I stray
    Vv. 2-3 as text; attrib-
    uted to "Hook"?

189 [Untitled]
    Je ne vous dira
    3 staves (2 treble and
    bass); v. 2 as text.

190 The Lass of Richmond Hill
    On Richmond Hill there
    lives a lass
    Vv. 2-3 as text.

192 Sweet Girl Can You Love Me
    Dear Nancy I've sailed
    the world all around
    Vv. 2-3 as text.

Page

194 The Cottage in the Grove.
    Composed by Mr. Hook
    Now wanton gales perfume
    the glade
    Vv. 2-3 as text.

196 The Heaving of the Lead, by
    Shield
    For England when with a
    fav'ring gale
    Vv. 2-3 as text.

197 The Caledonian Maid. Composed
    by I. Moulds, written
    by P. Pindair
    Oh say have you my Mary
    seen the Caledonian maid
    Vv. 2-3 as text.

199 [Blank]

200 Adams and Liberty
    Ye sons of Columbia who
    bravely have fought
    Vv. 2-9 as text.

202 The March of the Samnites, with
    Variations
    For keyboard alone.

207 Sonatas by Eichner
    For keyboard alone.

215 [Untitled]
    End of unidentified song;
    v. 2 as text.

216 The Mermaids Song. A Canzonett
    by Haydn
    Now the dancing sun beams
    play
    V. 2 as text.

[1] Rousseaus Dream
    For keyboard alone;
    attributed to B. Cramer.

11. *DISTRICT OF COLUMBIA: WASHINGTON. LIBRARY OF CONGRESS, MUSIC DIVISION. MT356.C62 CASE.*

MUSIC BOUND AT THE END OF A VOLUME OF FIVE TUTORS FOR FIFE, FLUTE, OR VIOLIN. [40] pp. 17 x 23 cm.

20th-century binding in half-leather and

marble paper over boards. Pages numbered
on rectos only.

Entries in same hand; probably in same ink
and on same paper

Inscription: "Edward Murphey, Newport, October
26, 1790," on original flyleaf now pasted
inside front cover.

All the tutors were published in London; the
first is the

> Entire New and Compleat Instructions for
> the Fife, Containing the Best and Easiest
> Directions to Learn That Instrument with
> a Collection of the Most Celebrated Marches,
> Airs, &c. Performed in the Guards & Other
> Regiments. NB: The Tunes in This Book are
> proper for the German Flute. London,
> Printed by Longman and Broderip, No. 26
> Cheapside. Price: 2 s.

Melody only, in treble clef, without words.

Page [*Verso* pagination supplied]   Page [*Verso* pagination supplied]

1 The Ranting Highlander
   The Lads of the Village
   I'll Towzel Your Kurchy

2 The Lad with a White Cockade
   Careless Sally
   Taylor Dun Over
   The Dusty Miller

3 For A That & A That
   Auld Robin Gray

4 [Untitled]
   Rural Felicity
   Chaises Retreat

5 The 71 Regiments Quickstep
   Lads and Lasses
   March in *The God of Love*

6 Thomsons Quick Step
   Quick Time
   Free Masons March

7 Green Grows the Rushes
   The Galley Slave

8 The Minors of Wicklow

Capt. Reads March
The Rakes of Marlow
Black Marys Hornpipe

9 Bung Your Eye
   Ca ira

10 To Arms
    Adagio
    Quick Time
    Colledge Hornpipe

11 Friend and Pitcher
    Marseilles Hymn

12 Rosline Castle
    Quick Time Old Continental
       March

13 Black Joke
    Jollity
    Old Buffs Quick Step

14 La Damoiselle
    Free Masons March
    Mrs. Blairs Reel
    Maid of the Mill

11. *DISTRICT OF COLUMBIA: WASHINGTON. LIBRARY OF CONGRESS (EDWARD MURPHEY)*

Page [*Verso* pagination supplied]   Page [*Verso* pagination supplied]

15   Succesful Campign
     The 15 Regiments Quick Step
     Polonese Dance

16   Yankey Doodle
     Last Sunday Morn I Sail
        from Cork
     Good Morrow to Your Night
        Cap

17   The Ladys Play Thing or
        General Hows March
     The Oysterwifes Rant
     The 17 Regiments Quick Step

18   Lillys of France
     King George the Second March
     Jacks Favourwright

19   Peggy and Molly
     Willys Rare and Willys Fair

20   The Bells of Newport
     Nancy Dorson [i.e. Dawson]
     Retreat
     The Drums Call

21   Well Gang Nae Mair to Yon Town
     Bunker Hill

22   General Washingtons March
     Bellisle March
     Welcome Here Again

23   New French March
     Peggy Bon

24   Presidents New March
     Boston March

25   Down the Burn and Through
        the Mead
     My Dog & My Gun
     Over the Water to Charley

26   The Banks of the Dee
     St. Partrix Day in the
        Morning
     The New Riged Ship

27   The Troopers Quick Step
     The 8th Regiments Quick March
     Had the Lass Til I Win
        at Her

28   Troop
     The High Landers March
     The Buff Coat

29   You the Point or I Am in Love
        with Twenty
     French March
     The Rost Beef of Old England

30   Anacreon in Heaven
     The Ladys Breast Knot
     A Favourite Jigg

31   Before I Was Married
     The Lee Rigg
     Dance in *Queen Mab*

32   A Hornpipe
     Over the Hills and Far Away
     The Flowers of Edin Burgh

33   Scotch Grays March
     The Grand Parade
     Mrs. Katy Halls Reel

34   Bow, Wow Wow
     York Fusiliers

35   The Royal Glasgow Volunteers
        Jigg
     Majors Maggot
     Cottilion

36   The Celebrated Slow Movt. in
        Pleyels Concerte
     I'm like a Skiff on the Ocean
        Tost
     Black Sloven

37   Bakers Hornpipe
     Robi Down
     The Corporal

38   The Ball
     Giga or A Jigg
     The New German Spa

39   Carlen Is Your Daughter Ready
     A Yankey Reveily
     The Widows Rant

40   British Granider
     The Irish Girl
     Off She Goes
        Above the last line of music is
        written, "The End of My Song."

12. *DISTRICT OF COLUMBIA: WASHINGTON. LIBRARY OF CONGRESS, MUSIC DIV-*
ISION. ML96.R28 CASE.

"REINAGLE: SONATAS FOR THE PIANOFORTE." 68 pp.
31 cm.

Binder's spine title; 20th-century binding in
blue half-leather and marbled paper over boards.
Foliation at margins; pagination on binding
tapes.

All entries in composer's hand; same ink and paper.

Inscriptions: attributions indicated by cataloger,
pp. 13-23.

Described by Sonneck-Upton, p. 393, and in more
detail by Ernest C. Krohn in "Alexander Reinagle
as Sonatist," including a facsimile of p. 62
(opposite p. 147). That Krohn did not know the
source of the two sets of variations has been
shown by Robert E. Hopkins, to whom we are
indebted for the attributions below. His edition
of Reinagle's sonatas is published in the series,
Recent Researches in American Music, vol. 5;
individual sonatas and excerpts have been published
in various anthologies of American music.

Page

1 Sonata. Piano Forte. A.
   Reinagle. Philadelphia.
   i.e., title-page for
   the following:

2 Sonata I
   In D major.

12 [Blank]

13 [Tema con variazioni]
    In A major; p. 16 is
    blank, but added overlays
    include alternate versions
    of cadential sections.
    Title in brackets and
    attributions to Haydn
    and to Reinagle in pencil
    in cataloger's hand.
    This is the second move-
    ment of Haydn's Symphony
    in D major (H.I:53),
    "L'Impérial," transcribed
    possibly by Reinagle for
    piano, perhaps intended
    for violin accompaniment.

Page

19 [Tema con variazioni] A. Reinagle
    In D major; includes one
    alternate overlay. Title
    in brackets and attrib-
    ution to Reinagle in
    pencil in cataloger's hand.
    This is an arrangement,
    apparently with violin
    accompaniment (part now
    lost), of Reinagle's
    Maggy Lauder variations
    published in Philadelphia
    in 1787 in his *A Selec-
    tion of the Most Favor-
    ite Scots Tunes with
    Variations.*

24 [Blank]

25 [Blank]

26 [Blank]

27 Sonata. Piano Forte. A.
    Reinagle
    i.e., Title-page for the
    following:

13. *DISTRICT OF COLUMBIA: WASHINGTON. LIBRARY OF CONGRESS (ABEL SHATTUCK)*

Page

28 Sonata II
      In E major; pp. 34-35
      blank.

44 Sonata
      In F major.

Page

53 [Blank]

54 Sonata III
      In C major.

13. *DISTRICT OF COLUMBIA: WASHINGTON. LIBRARY OF CONGRESS, MUSIC DIVISION. M63.S5 CASE.*

"A. SHATTUCKS BOOK." 114 pp. 11 x 19 cm.

Cover title: "A. Shattuck."

Bound in brown leather with newspaper pasted inside front and back covers. P. 101 omitted in pagination.

Entries in different hands and inks, but on same paper.

Inscription: "Abel Shattuck," p. [2].

Probably for fife; melody only, unless otherwise indicated.

Page

3 The River
   Hob or Nob

4 The Wood Cutter
   The Freemasons March

5 Maid in the Pump Room
   Quick March

6 New Pump Room
   Now or Never

7 No. 13, or Fifer's Delight
   The Black Sloven

8 Capt. Reeds March
   The Old Woman

9 My Love She Is ...
   March On

10 Greenfield
   Paddy Whack

Page

11 This Absence Will Not
      Alter Me
   Double Dutch

12 The Miller
   Friendship

13 The Dukes March
   My Dog & My Gun
   The White Cockade

14 The Fifers Fancy
   Lullees Croacker
   Wanderer

15 Lees Uncle
   Longolee

16 The Old Man
   The Hollow Drum

17 Buttonhole
   Trip to Pluckman
   My Troop

Page

Page		Page	
18	Rooling Hornpipe The Girl I Left Behind Me Yankey Doodle		Mananio The Millers Asleep in His Mill
19	Stones Grindall A Reel Duke Hulisetons March	34	The Lemon Charley Bumbo Seconds to On the Road to Boston
20	Prants Jig Bald Hilander The Liberty Tree	35	Granoe's March 2 treble parts.
21	The Bells of Norwich I Wish I May Die If I Do	36	Rural Felicity Philadelphia March Baron Stuben's Favorite
22	The Successful Champaign A Quick Step A Retreat	37	The Fishers Hornpipe Stepneys Hornpipe
23	The Ladies Dance The Rogues March Money in Both Pockets	38	Charley Over the Water
24	The Germans Pane King Williams March	39	The General The Ragged Jacket The Drummer's Call
25	Fifer's Master-peace Prince Eugeens March Wild Irish	40	The Haymaker's Charley Over the Water The Young Widow
26	The French Troop Ye Social Powers	41	March of the 13th Regament Hen's March
27	A Quick Step Jefferson & Liberty The Black Bird	42	The Lively Girl Things ____[illegible] Reel Up and Down
28	Yankee Doodle New Queen of Hearts The Rolling Hornpipe	43	Soldiers Joy Irish Washerwoman Over the Moor
29	General Washingtons March The Second to General Washingtons March	44	Boury Wood Over the Hills and Vallies Gone The Devil Untied
30	Corus Gig Yankee Doodle New	45	The Challenge Bob and Joan Humours of Glyn
31	The British Grenadiers March 2 parts (treble and bass). Jefferson's March	46	The Corn Planters Swiss Guards March
32	The Generals Salute Boston March The Scotch Grail	47	Elbow Room Washingtons March The Woodcock
33	Greens March	48	Grenadiers March Scotch Duty Lagorrs Wake[?]

13. *DISTRICT OF COLUMBIA: WASHINGTON. LIBRARY OF CONGRESS (ABEL SHATTUCK)*

Page

Page

81 As I Was Going to Negro Hill
    Love For Eaver

82 Hornpipe Gervot in Otho –
        from Holyoke
    The British Grenadiers
    Patty Kisses Sweet

83 As I Was Going to Baltimore
    In the City of London There
        Lived a Maid
    Peas Straw

84 [Blank]

85 Balidiner March
    Cullodon Fight

86 [Blank]

87 Lady Bruces Reel
        2 parts (treble and
        bass).
    No Luck About the House

88 This Is None of My House
    Real of Six
    Apples for Ladies
    Worcester March

89 The Four Seasons
    The Royal March

90 Ross Castle
    Loneac
    New York Beuty

91 Lady Bairds Reel
    None So Pretty
    Kiss Me Quicickly

92 The Motm[?] Grove
    None So Pretty
    Hendricks Reel
    A Reel by P. R.

93 Federal Reel
    The Lover of Flowers
    Frenship
        2 treble parts.
    Black Dance

94 The Bank of Flowers
    Fresh & Strong
        2 parts (treble and bass)

    The Unhappy Swain
        3 parts (2 treble and
        bass).

95 Druncan House
    Jemmy & Nancy
    The Red Joak
    Wet & Weary Junr.
    Lady and Lasses

96 Midnight Ramble
    Go to the Devil and Shake
        Yourself
    The Devil's Dream

97 Humours of Glynn
        2 parts (treble and bass).
    The Sergeant's Delight
    Favorite

98 Mann's Hornpipe
        2 parts (treble and bass).
    Quick March

99 The Hunters of the Alps
    The Padys Resort
    The Toad

100 Jemmy O Flanigen
    Slow March
    Hornpipes Pipe

102 French Quick March
    Quick March
    Woods Hornpipe
    Hornpipe

103 A Hornpipe
    The Werth Hornpipe
    Rudleam Hornpipe

104 Hornpipe
    Colledge Hornpipe

105 Reveilly
    General
    To Arms
    Doublings of the Tattoo
    Devils Dance
    The Irish Devil

106 Officers Dinner Drum
    Troop for the Colours
    The Gathering

14. *ILLINOIS: CHICAGO. NEWBERRY LIBRARY. CASE MS VM 1450 M29.*

COPYBOOK OF DANCE TUNES. 179 pp., [12] leaves
20 x 16.5 cm.

> Bound in leather over paper boards; newer
> leather sewn over the old on spine; one thick
> signature, followed by one loose signature
> in oblong format, sewn at top edge. Pagi-
> nation in compiler's hand; lacking pp. 1-4,
> 35-36, 39-40, 65-66, 95-96, 119-20, 129-30,
> 178; pp. 5-8 now bound after p. 179.
>
> Both signatures in same hand throughout,
> probably that of John Carroll (see inscrip-
> tions below), who is also cited as composer
> of works on pp. 31, 32, 78, 126, 142-43, [Bv].
> Same ink throughout first signature except
> for emendations as noted.
>
> Inscriptions: "John Carroll, Fort N[iagra]"
> and "Bequeathed to S. DeVeaux by John Carroll,
> Nov. 1812," inside front cover; "October
> the 10th 1804," p. 142; "John Carroll," p. [Ev].
>
> A Scale for the Fiddle, inside front cover.
>
> For treble melody instrument (violin or flute),
> unless otherwise noted. This MS shares a

repertory somewhat similar to Whittier
Perkins' book (MS No. 37 below).

Page

5 The High Road to Dublin
Hessian Camp
The Nose Gay
The Leno
The Pigmy

6 The Pockett
Moncy in Both Pockets
The Attorney
Captain McKay's Fancy

7 Trip It up Stairs
Give Round the World
Hunting the Hare
No Time to Loose [sic]
The Rigg'd Ship

8 Miss Robinson's Fancy
The Rosetta
Ye Social Powers
The Four Seasons

9 Paddy Whack
The Sicilian Peasant °
Drummond Castle
Open the Door to Thee
The Humours of Clana Cilty

10 The Humours of Kilkenny
You May Say That
The Mirtle Grove
The Young Widdow

11 The Humours of Fort Hammilton
The Idler
Flush the Cat from Under the
Table
Do John Let Me Alone
First two words added
later.

12 The Devil [crossed through]
Gang We Yon
Batchelors Hall
Do Be Quiet
Stoney Point
Dribs of Brandy

13 Jackson's Dream
Jack with His Hairy Cap
The Padlock

Page

Choice of Harlequin
Pray Let Me Alone

14 Rakes of Kilkenny
The Irish Mans a Wattle
Hudibrass
Dunfries House
The Munster Lass

15 When I Followed a Lass
M. O'Blany
The Contented Man
Miller's Rant
The Humours of Rovetta
Lucy's Country Dance

16 Sally Magee
The Critick
The Rover
The Merry Month Hounds
Pither in Enough

17 O Dear Polly
Go to the Devil & Shake
Yourself
Moll in the Wadd
The Context
The Rights of Women

18 Lord Dupline's Jigg
Lough Seven Side

19 Huntington Castle
Miss Douglas Brighton's Jigg
The Presedent
The Dutchess

20 Humours of Bandon
New Jersey
The Innocent Maid
The New Fandango

21 The Old Woman
The Green Shades of Gask
Roguara Doo
Rackman's Rant

22 The Sooner the Better
Morgan Rattler
Married & Nood & Naw

23 Larry Grogan
Rural Fellicity

Page

45 Cameron's Frolick
Miss Jone's Reel
Grant's Rant
Alliance - A Cotillion
The Bottle and Glass
The Orange Tree

46 Old Wife Beyond the Fire
Delia's Birth Night
The Ale Wife & Her Barrel
Mode of Montreal
The Little Plough Boy

47 Widdow Dickens Country Dance
Mary Gray
The Victory
Jonny Give Her Thou Thing
Go & Come

48 The Husband Must Rule
Wife: No No That Can't Be I
    in My Turn
Gossop, for Peace Sake
    Half It
Willy Was a Wanton Wag

49 The Bonny Lass of Aberdeen
The Fond Pair
Bob's Hornpipe
Love in a Village

50 Let Love Be the Toast
The Belfast Voluntiers
The White Hair'd Lad for Me
Mirth & Joy
Come Boys Drink About

51 Lyra
The Twadele
Cate & Davy
Peas Upon a Trencher

52 Hobson's Choice
The Orange Grove
The Bottom of the Punch
    Bowl

53 Braes of Aughtertire
The Grand Spye
The Successful Campaign
McDonald's Rant

54 The Highland Man Kiss'd
    His Mother

Page

Shay's March
The Hermitage
The Savage Dance
Rickard's Hornpipe

55 Jonny's Baisbee
The Girl I Left Behind Me
Miss Hunter's Hornpipe
The Bed of Roses

56 Lough Arick Side
Navel Review
1st Regt Quick March
The Irishman's Kiss

57 Fanny's Toy
Robinson's Hornpipe
Fisher's Hornpipe
The Brave Yanco Boys

58 Saunder's Second Hornpipe
Madam Hilligsberg's Reel
Richer's Hornpipe
You May If You Will

59 Care Thou Canker
The Humours of Boston
The Merry Dancers
Cotillion La Constance

60 Cotillion Little Wood
York Fusaliers
Corn Planter

61 The Tea Pot
Alemande Franedue [i.e.,
    Française]
Capt. Francis Wemyss Strathpey
The Briefe Meeting

62 Capt. Francis Wemyss Delight
Mr. David McDowal's Stratspey
The Honble Miss Rolles Reel
Sweet Apples
What the Devil Ails You

63 The Lass of Richmond Hill
Capt. O'Bosvil's March
Lovely Molly
Fife Hunt - A Favourit Dance

64 Dutches of York's Fancy
Huss Hills - A Hornpipe
Cumberland House
Bonny Jane

14. ILLINOIS: CHICAGO. NEWBERRY LIBRARY (JOHN CARROLL)

Page

Page

67 The Dueler
    What a Beau Your Granny Was
    He's Aye a Kissing Me
    There's Nae Luck About the
        House
    Push About the Jarum

68 The Bow Wow Wow
    Dans votre lit
    Frog & Mouse
    Row Dow Dow
    A Soldier Is the Lad for Me

69 The Sprig of Myrtle
    The Duenna
    Batchelors of Every Station
    The Devil's Dream

70 Mason's Laddie
    The Parting Kiss
    Alass Poor Cate
    None So Pretty

71 Lady Baird's Reel
    Duke of Gordon's Birthday
    Peggy Perkins
    Lucy Campbell Afternoon

72 Durang's Hornpipe
    Careless Sally
    Boston March
    German March

73 Johnson's Fancy
    Jenny's Fancy
    O Dear Mamma
    Cannada Farewell
    Oxford Camp

74 A French Air
    This Is None of My House
    Miss West's Favourite
    Not Fond of Poverty
    The Bea[u]ty of the World for
        the Pipe
        In different ink. See
        also p. 75 below.

75 For Ever Fortune
    When First I Slipt My
        Leading Strings
    Cynthia
    The Beauty of the World
        See also p. 74 above.

    The Old Woman's Orratory

76 German Dance
    My Little Doll
    The Rose Bud

77 The Blue Bell of Scotland
    Green Witch Hill
    Capt. Triumphant
    The Lilly
    Fany's Fancy

78 Lucy's Delight
    Parker's Wish
    Bennet's Reel
    Majr Porter's Fancy by Carroll
    Pompey Ran Away

79 Sally's Favourite Country
        Dance
    Lady Townsend's Fancy
    The Bastil
    The New Fair
    Wilke's Fancy
    The New Highland Laddy

80 The Rope Dance
    Felton's Gavot

81 Boudinor's Concert

82 The Seasons - A Favourite
        Country Dance
    Pomalia the Blue Bird
    A French Dance
    The Honey Moon

83 The Fair American
    The Little Island
    The Black Wall Nut

84 The Iannessy Reel
    The Straw Berry
    Tom Tollese's Hornpipe
    Larry O'Brian

85 The Wonder
    The Runaway
    The Queen's Short Troop

86 The Lads of Dunce
    The Magazine
    My Wife's a Wanton Wee Thing
    Shilinagigg

Page

Page

87   Let the Toast Pass
      O'Derige's Hornpipe
      Whistle Over the Levet

88   The Cuckoo's Nest
      The Favourite Mock Cuckow Solo

89   The Grape Vine

90   The Pink
      The Nun in Her Teens
      The Handsome Daughter
      McKays Fancy
      The Poppet Dance

91   The Brisk Widdow
      The Little Wanderer
      A New Quick Step

92   Capt. Johnson's Billiard Table
      Jackson's Toast
      The Blue Bonnet, Sally Baked a
            Pudding
      Jump Up Jane
      Coming Home From the Wake

93   O My Little Saylor Boy
      The Prim Rose
      La Visite

94   The Grand Spie
      Kitty's Ramble to Youghil
      Grand Spie
            Variant of the above.

97   Philadelphia March
      March for the Appollo Lodge
      Caty's a Beauty

98   March in *The God of Love*
      Col. Read's 1st March

99   Col. Read's 2d March
      Capt. Blomberg's March
      The 16th Regt. March

100   Col. Prevost March of the
            60 Regt.
      Prince Ferdinand's March
      The March in the Athradates

101   Genl Lamberton's, or the
            68th Regt. March
      Northumberland March
      Genl Washington's March

102   President's New March
      Handle's Trumpet
      The 15th Regt. March

103   London March
      Col. Horn's March
      March in the Battle of Prague

104   Genl Kniphausens March
      Lord McDonnald's March
      Lord Gore's March
      March Debose
            Same as p. 108 below.

105   1st Cole Stream March
      Philadelphia March
      Rhode Island March

106   Guardian Angels
      My Nanny O
      Janessary's March

107   Capt. Houghton's March
      Capt. Read's March
      New Port March

108   The Irish Volunteers March
      March Debose
            Same as p. 104 above.
      Morellis March
      2nd Cole Stream March

109   Bonaparte's 1st March
      Bonaparte's 2d March

110   Bonaparte's 3d March
      Miss Abington
      The President's March

111   The Tear
      Catherine Ogee
      The Kilkenny Rangers' March

112   The French Grenadiers March
      Hail Collumbia, The President's
            Favourite March
      Barron Stuben's March

113   The Turks March

114   A Favourite March
      Lord Antrim's March
      Gilderoy

115   Duke of York's March
      Sylvia the Fair

Page

Page

Page

Page

170 I Sold a Guiltless Negro Boy
Saturday Night at Sea
The Cheering Rosary

171 Solitary Air
First Strain i the Overature
of *The Desert* [er]
Signior La Clair's Minuet

172 Last Adieu
A Favourite Venetian
Ballad

173 My Bonny Lowland Laddie –
A Scotch Air
A Favourite Allamande

174 Alloa House
The Little Piece of Music
Duetto
[Primo] only.

175 Weideman's Minuet
Air de Julia
A French Song

176 The Oft Flowing Avon
Capt. Lam's Minuet
Lady Otway's Minuet
Prince Henry's Minuet

177 Beneath a Green Shade
Cotalin Trail
The Mill Mill O

179 Past 12 O'Clock
Yomam a Knuck
Auld Robin Gray
La Lumiere

[Ar] Sandy over the See
Sweet Transports Gentle
Wishes Go
He Stole My Tender Heart
Away
The word "Collin" appears
in the left hand margin.

[Av] Woman, War, and Wine
Battle first my soul
imploys
Title nearly all
trimmed away.

[Br] Durang's Hornpipe

The Galley Slave
Quick Step

[Bv] Fort Niagra Quick Step by
Carroll

[Cr] Minuet 1st
Minuet 2nd

[Cv] A Favourite March
Crossed through.

[Dr] Lord Antrim's March
The Infant Cucow

[Dv] March in *Henry the 4th*

[Er] A Solo for the Fife
Secondo for the Solo
Both constituting a
duet for fifes.

[Ev] [Blank]

[Fr] Hunt the Squirrel
Peggy Perkins

[Fv] [Blank]

[Gr] Dobney's Grand March
Royal Quick Step
Duke of Gordon's Birthday

[Gv] [Blank]

[Hr] Chaunt civvige [i.e., Chant
civique?]
Hearts of Oak
Lady Baird's Reel

[Hv] [Blank]

[Ir] Faithful Shepperdess
Nicolai's Favourite Rondo
None So Pretty

[Iv] [Blank, except for illegible
scribbling]

[Jr] Alass Poor Cate
When First I Saw the Grace-
ful Move
Mary's Dream
The Parting Kiss

[Jv] [Contains accounting of
shingles and clapboarding,
and some scribbling.]

Page   Page

[K*r*] How Happy's the Soldier Who
      Lives on his Pay
   The Duenna
   Poor Darby
   Anna

[K*v*] The White Bull
     Baltimore

[L*r*] [List, crossed through, of
     "Men in the Quarter Masters
     Employ in the [Marines?]."]

15. *ILLINOIS: CHICAGO. NEWBERRY LIBRARY. CASE MS -VM1.M295.*

COPYBOOK OF KEYBOARD MUSIC AND SONGS. 47 [i.e. 48] leaves. 23 x 28 cm.

Three-quarter leather with marbled paper over boards. Leaf 19 numbered twice.

Entries in similar handwriting except for "Ingle Side" (leaf 43[*r*]), and on same paper in different inks.

Inscriptions: "M. T. Leddel," on leather label on center of front cover; "Mrs. Mary Latham," pencilled inside front cover. Pencilled **dates**, both referring to dates of events cited in titles: "1813," leaf 20[*v*]; "1804," leaf 26[*r*].

Arthur F. Schrader correctly points out that a number of other titles, particularly those near the end of the MS, seem to have first appeared in the late 1820s. The MS has nevertheless been included because of the many 18th-century titles it contains.

Foliation [*Recto* and *verso* supplied]   Foliation [*Recto* and *verso* supplied]

1*r* Dull care
    What Can the Matter Be
    The Sun Sets at Night

1*v* The Cuckoo
    Now the sun is in the west
     3 vv.

2*r* Life Let Us Cherish
    Bunker Hill
     Why should vain mortals

2*v* The Fall of Paris - Allegro
    Cheering Rosary - Dolce

3*r* [Blank]

3*v* Fishers Hornpipe
    The Portugues Hymn
     Hither ye faithful haste

    with songs of triumph
     3 vv.

4*r* La belle Catherine
    Shepherds I Have Lost My Love
     Shepherds I have lost my love

4*v* Henry's Cottage Maid

5*r* Fresh and Strong, a Favorite
     Song - Andante
    Fresh and strong

5*v* Overture to *The Desert*[er] -
    Allegro non troppo

6*v* The Battle of the Nile
    Arise, arise Britannia's sons
    Only first line of text
    inscribed.

Foliation [*Recto* and *verso* supplied]   Foliation [*Recto* and *verso* supplied]

7r   Oh Whistle and I Will Come
  to You My Lad
   Oh whistle and I will come
  to you my lad

7v   The Request – Andante
   Tell me babling Eccho
  Faint and Wearily the Worn
   Traveller – Allegro
   moderate
   Faint and wearily the worn
  traveller

8r   Nicolai's Rondo

8v   Windsor Park – Rondo
  allegretto

10r The Irish Washerwoman

10v See from Ocean Rising –
  Moderato
   See from ocean rising
   Duet from *Paul and
   Virginia*; two sections
   so marked.

11r The Soldier's Joy

11v Bonaparte's March

12r Bonnie Doon, a Favorite Scotch
  Song – Andante
   Ye banks and braes of
   Bonnie Doon
   2 vv.

12v Molly Put the Kettle On –
  A Favorite Rondo – Allegro

13v Paddy O'Rafferty – Allegretto

15r Washington's March
  Portugal – CM
   Sweet is thy work my God
   Textual incipit only.

15v A Favorite Waltz

16r The Rose Tree

16v The New President's March
  The Galley Slave

17r Rosline Castle

17v Caravane's March in *The*

Forty Theives
A French Cotillion

18r College Hornpipe
  Haste to the Wedding

18v Saxon March – Moderate
  manestoso

19r Boston March
  White Cockade

19v Down the Burn Davie Love

19Ar My Ain Kind Dearie –
  Moderately andante
  With six variations.

20v A Votive Wreath to the Memory
  of Capt. J. Lawrence
  Tho' o'er him swell the
  fun'ral mound
  4 vv.

21r Dorchester March

21v The Coronach, or Funeral Song,
  from *The Lady of the
  Lake* – Andante affettuoso
  quarer larghtto
  He's gone on the mountain
  3 vv. written out with
  accompaniment; ritornello
  varies slightly.

22v Hob Nob

23r Lochinvar, Written by Walter
  Scott
   Oh young Lochinvar is come

23v Columbia
  China

24r Denmark – LM – Moderato
  Before Jehovah's awful
  throne

25r The Indian Philosopher
  Why should our joys trans-
  form to pain?
  Adams and Liberty
  Ye sons of Columbia

25v Bristol March

26r Bonapartes Coronation March

Foliation [*Recto* and *verso* supplied]   Foliation [*Recto* and *verso* supplied]

26*v*   To the Brook & the Willow
        To the brook & the willow
        2 vv.

27*r*   Friendship
        Paddy Carey, a Cotillion

27*v*   Listen to the Voice of Love
        O listen to the voice of
        love
        3 vv.

28*r*   Is There a Heart That Never
        Lov'd, Sung by Mr.
        Braham
        Is there a heart that
        never lov'd
        2 vv.

28*v*   Strike the Cymbel - Allegro
        Strike the cymbal
        Anthem, alternating
        treble solo and duet with
        4-part chorus; with
        keyboard accompaniment.

31*r*   Overature to *Oscar and*
        Malvina, with The High-
        land March Orchestral
        instrumentation noted;
        continued on leaves 36*r*-
        37*r* below.

34*r*   Dunkeld House
        The Sicilian Hymn
        O sanctissima purissima
        dulcis Virgo Maria

34*v*   Blue Ey'd Mary - Andante
        Tell me blue ey'd stranger
        2 vv.

35*r*   I Have Loved Thee Dearly
        Loved Thee
        I have loved thee dearly
        loved thee
        2 vv.

35*v*   Pleyel's Hymn - Second - C.M.
        While there I seek pro-
        tecting power

36*r*   [Continuation of Overature to
        Oscar and Malvina]
        Continued from leaf 31*r*

        above; sections marked
        Highland March, March
        Battle Piece, and The
        Caledonian Hunt.

37*v*   Swiss Waltz - Moderato
        Theme and three variations.

39*v*   Tho' Love Is Warm Awhile,
        Composed by Braham -
        Andantinos
        Tho love is warm awhile
        2 vv.

40*r*   Retirement - CM
        While thee I seek protect-
        ing power

40*v*   Hark the Goddess Diana
        Hark the goddess Diana
        Treble duet with keyboard
        accompaniment; 2 vv.

41*v*   Bruce's Address to His Army,
        a Scotch Song
        Scots wha hae wi' bellace
        3 vv.

42*r*   Oh Say Not Woman's Heart
        Is Bought
        Oh say not woman's heart
        is bought
        3 vv.

42*v*   Yankee Doodle
        Mark Me Alfred - Andante

43*r*   Morpeth's March
        The Ingle Side
        It's rare to see the
        morning breeze

43*v*   Troubadour
        Gaily the troubadour touched
        his guitar
        3 vv. as text.

44*r*   Absence - Andante
        Days of absence I am weary
        The Merry Swiss Girl

44*v*   The Monkey's Wedding
        The monkey married the
        baboon's sister
        The Cheat - Lively

15. *ILLINOIS: CHICAGO. NEWBERRY LIBRARY (M. T. LEDDEL)*

Foliation [*Recto* and *verso* supplied] Foliation [*Recto* and *verso* supplied]

45*r* The Rose of Allandale
     The morn was fair the
     skies were clear
       4 vv., the last in pencil

46*r* The Spanish Patriot's March
    The Last Link Is Broken
    The last link is broken
      2 vv.

47*v* Hours There
     Hours there were to
     memry dear
      Copied upside down
      in different ink;
      3 vv.

16. *ILLINOIS: CHICAGO. NEWBERRY LIBRARY. CASE MS VM 1 S381M.*

"CHARLOTTE L. SCHROPP'S MUSIC BOOK. 7TH MARCH
1800." [32] pp. 17.5 x 24.5 cm.

Title from front cover.

Bound in thin paper boards.

Entries by different hands but on same
paper.

Contains eight songs in English and eleven
in German, for one or two voices and bass
(keyboard). All are sacred, except for those
listed below.

Page [Pagination supplied]   Page [Pagination supplied]

1-2 Moderata par Foose
    When the rosy morn
    appearing.
      For 1 or 2 treble voices
      and keyboard.

30-31 Anna's **Lute**. Words by Henry
      J. L. White. Affectuoso.
    Yes once more that dying
    strain
      Treble and bass duet with
      keyboard; vv. 2-3 as
      text.

17. *ILLINOIS: CHICAGO. NEWBERRY LIBRARY. CASE MS VM 290 N91.*

"FLUTE AND VIOLIN. 1795 [1799 CROSSED THROUGH]-
1800." 64 [i.e., 66] leaves. 31 cm.

Title from front cover; at head of title:
"Flute."

Bound in worn leather over boards. Leaves
have been renumbered in pencil in later hand
according to present contents, without regard

for leaves missing from previous numbering (in ink) which ends at leaf 43. Leaves 10 and 42 have been inserted; additional leaf between leaves 45 and 46 and following leaf 64. Lacking leaves 12r-14v, 22r-24v, 38 (all from previous numbering).

Entries in at least three different hands and in different inks but on same kind of paper.

Inscriptions: "L[evi] Shepherd," front cover; "March 7, 1795," leaf 8v; "Thos. Shepherd N H 26th Octr 1795," leaf 15r; "Bonney March 11 1796," leaf 16r; "April 19th 1796," leaf 16v; "Franc^s Wilkinson, Sept. 4th, 1800, Newfoundland,"leaf 36v; "London, March 1800," leaf 50v; "London 19th March 1800,"leaf 52v; "Levi Shepherd's friend [i.e., Wilkinson] Sep 4, 1800, upon the sea," leaf 56v; "F. W. Sept. 4th 1800, wrote at sea," leaf 60v; Fran^s Wilkinson, Sept. 4th 1800," leaf [65r].

Melody only, unless otherwise indicated. Music copied only on rectos of leaves; versos contain poetry and some song-texts.

Leaf [Showing present numbering; earlier numbering in parentheses]

Leaf [Showing present numbering; earlier numbering in parentheses]

1-3 [Prose, poetry, or blank with ruled staves.]

4 (3r) Flowers of the Forest. Slow
Bonnie Charlie
Fair Hebe

5 (4r) Gamachree My Molly
My Fond Shepherd
Broom of the Cowden Knows. Slow
Thou Soft Flowing Avon by Thy Silver Streams
Brisk Young Drummer

6 (5r) Lass with a Delicate Air
Morgan Rattler. Jigg.
A Hunting Song
42nd Regt's March
Lovely Nymphe

7 (6r) Langan Frater. Slow.
The Plough Boy

The Peacock
Heaving the Anchor

8 (7r) Fisher's Minuet
Lady Coventry's Minuet
2 parts.
Down the Burn Davie
When trees did bud and fields were green
Words as text, leaf 6v.

9 (8r) How Sweet through the Woodlands
How sweet in the woodlands
2 parts; words as text, leaf 7v.
Flowers of Edingburgh
Dorsetshire March

10([8a]r) How Imperfect Is Expression
How imperfect is expression
2 parts; words as text, leaf 9v.

(51)

Leaf [Showing present numbering; earlier numbering in parentheses]

Leaf [Showing present numbering; earlier numbering in parentheses]

11 (9r) Swiss Grards March
   2 parts.
   When Bidden to the Wake
   or Fair

12 (10r) A Favorite French March
   2 parts.

13 (11r) Roslin Castle

14 (15r) Ciara [?]
   Scotch Luck
   2 parts.
   Oxford to the Pantheon
   2 parts.

15 (16r) Maid of the Oak
   The Black Bird
   2 parts.
   The Sailor's Dream

16 (17r) Handel's Clarinet Duet
   2 parts.

17 (18r) York Fusileers Duet
   2 parts.

18 (19r) Gentle Cupid, for Two Ger.
   Flutes
   2 parts.
   Irish ____ ____[illegible]
   Flow
   2 parts (only "Primo"
   copied).

19 (20r) Grands March Duetto
   2 parts.

20 (21r) [Title lacking due to
   damaged page]
   2 parts.

21 (25r) The Wood Cutters Duetto
   2 parts.
   Scotch Air
   2 parts.

22 (26r) Magie Lawder
   Through the Wood Laddie

23 (27r) Lovely Nancy with Variations
   Includes two variations.
   Lady Coventry's Minuet
   2 parts.
   Cupid's Recruiting Seargent

24 (28r) Bellisle March Duet
   2 parts.
   Farewell ye Greenfields
   2 parts.

25 (29r) Prince Eugen's March Duet
   2 parts.
   Fetton's Gavot Duetto
   2 parts.

26 (30r) Marbrough Duetto
   2 parts.

27 (31r) Favorite, &c.
   Melony's Jigg

28 (32r) The Secilian Peasant
   Bath Medley
   Rain Water

29 (33r) Fitz Jame's Cotillion
   Franciscan Friar
   Charlotte McCarthy

30 (34r) The Dauphin Duet
   2 parts.
   Bank of Flowers

31 (35r) The Gilderoy Duetto
   2 parts.
   The Irish Billy

32 (36r) God Save Great Washington
   [crossed through]
   "George the Third,"
   written below "Wash-
   ington."
   New Lango Lee, or Banks of
   the Dee
   Aloa House, or The Shepherd Adonis
   The spring-time returns
   and clothes the green plain
   Words as text, leaf 43v.

33 (37[?]r)
   House Musick Duet
   2 parts; part of "Primo"
   mutilated.
   Grasshopper
   Little insect that on high
   Words as text, leaf 47v.

34 (39r) Air
   2 parts.

Leaf [Showing present numbering;   Leaf [Showing present numbering;
   earlier numbering in parentheses]   earlier numbering in parentheses]

	Washington's March	42 ([46a]*r*)
	Tawney Moor, Sung in *The*	
	Mountaineers	Fresh and Strong
		Fresh and strong the
35 (40*r*)	New Cold Stream March	breezes blowing
	Hunting Duetto by Ives, to	Words as text, leaf 41*v*.
	Which is Added Felton's	43 (47*r*) Anna, the Fear
	Gavotta	For Tenderness Form'd, Sung
	2 parts (only one copied).	in *The Heiress*
36 (41*r*)	Washington's 2[d] March	The Cottages
	Yankee Doodle	44 [Blank]
37 (42*r*)	The Watchful Pilot	45 Nancy Dawson
	For England When in	A Favorite Scotch Song. Slow
	Favoring Gale	Bricklayer. Country Dance
	2 parts (only "Primo"	A Free Mason's Song
	copied); words as text,	McPherson's Farewell
	leaf 46*v*.	Peter N[?]ealand's Gravity
38 (43*r*)	Henry's Cottage March	45a [Blank]
	2 parts.	46 [Blank]
	The Dispanding Negroe	47 For the German Flute. Duke of
39 (44*r*)	Quick March	York's March
	Air	Incomplete.
	Ma cher**e amie**	48 [Blank, or poetry]
	Ma chere amie, my charm-	55 [Untitled]
	ing fair	56 [Blank, or poetry]
40 (45*r*)	He Piped So Sweet [by] Hook	61 My Charming Sailor Boy
	Anna's Urn	Incomplete.
41 (46*r*)	I'd Think on Thee My Love	62 [Blank, or poetry]
	2 parts (only "Primo"	
	copied).	

18. *MARYLAND: FREDERICK. MARSHALL L. ETCHISON COLLECTION, C/O*
     MISS JOSEPHINE P. ETCHISON.

   COPYBOOK OF KEYBOARD MUSIC. [426] pp.
   9 x 16 cm.

      Handsewn into red and green floral cloth cover
      over boards.

      Entries in same hand (probably) and ink, and
      on same paper. Hand same or similar to MS
      No. 19.

      Inscriptions: "Thomas Schley, August the ____
      [remaining date illegible due to damage],"

18. MARYLAND: FREDERICK. MARSHALL L. ETCHISON COLLECTION (THOMAS SCHLEY 1)

inside back cover.

This MS is described and inventoried in "Church Music and Musical Life in Frederick, Maryland, 1745-1845," by Anne Louise Shifflet, pp. 13-16 and Appendix A. Schley (i.e., John Thomas Schley) was a church organist and music teacher who was born in Germany in 1712, emigrated to Maryland about 1739, and died there in 1790. It is possible, but not certain, that the MS is in his hand. A number of the later pieces did not become popular until after his death (e.g., "The President's March," p. [328], and the hymn-tune adaptation of Pleyel's melody, p. [305]). He is, however, listed as the composer of the organ preludes, pp. [110]-[33]. He is probably also the composer of the Sonatas I-X (pp. [164]-[80]) and the Lessons I-XVI (pp. [182]-[319]) since these are the same works attributed to him by title-page and position in the following MS (No. 19).

"These are Six Sorts of Notes in Music [i.e., keyboard rudiments]," pp. [1]-[8]. Lessons on Thoroughbass, pp. [287]-[90]. "The Art of Fingering the Piana Forte," p. [291]. "A Short Dictionary of Musical Terms [probably of Schley's devising]," p. [426].

For keyboard, unless otherwise indicated; specific instruments (harpsichord, pianoforte, or organ) are frequently cited in titles; six to twelve staves per page in spite of the MS's small size.

Page [Pagination supplied]

9	Malbrouk with Variations
12	The Welch Rabbit
13	French Country Dance Cotillion
14	The Staden Isleland Hornpipe
15	Nancy Dawson
16	Belile's March
17	The Cream Pot
18	Free Masons Tune
19	Lady Breastnot

Page [Pagination supplied]

20	Lady Coventrys Minuet
21	New Jersy
22	Largo: Preludio
23	Highland Reel
24	Gen: Washingtons March
25	The Pantheon Cotillion
26	La Belle Catharine, with Variations
28	Rosline Castle
29	Allegro, or, Coteree

Page [Pagination supplied]

276 Presto by Nicolai

280 A Favorite Lesson for the
      Piano-Forte

282 Overture, by Able

287 These Are the Figurs Used
      In Thorough Bass

288 Recapitulation of the Twelve
      Chords to Help the Memory

289 Thorough Bass, This Lesson,
      Containing All the Final
      Closes in Music

290 Thorough Bass, Made Easy

292 The Rose Tree
      A rose tree full in bearing
      V. 2 as text.

293 Little Bo Peep, by Mr. Hook
      Little Bo Peep has lost
      her sheep
      Vv. 2-3 as text.

294 O Dear What Can the Matter Be
      O dear what can the matter
      be
      V. 2 as text.

295 Sweet Rose, A New Song
      Yes yonder rose has sweet
      perfume
      Vv. 2-3 as text.

296 Dear Sally, A New Song
      Sweet lilly of the valley
      Vv. 2-3 as text.

297 Life Let Us Cherish
      Life let us cherish
      Vv. 2-3 as text.

298 Somebody
      Where [i.e., Were] I
      oblig'd to beg my bread
      Vv. 2-3 as text.

300 The Dusky Night
      The dusky night rides down
      the sky
      Vv. 2-6 as text.

Page [Pagination supplied]

302 Sternes Maria
      Twas near a thickets calm
      retreat
      Vv. 2-3 as text.

304 Brunswick, with the Enterludes
      To thee O God my cries
      Lenox
      Lord of worlds above

305 German Hymn, by Pleyel, with
      the Enterlud's
      Children of the heav'nly
      King
      Vv. 2-3 as text.

306 Hanover Tune, with the Enter-
      lud's

307 Easter Hymn

308 The 100 Psalm, with the
      Enterlud's

309 Coleshill, or Dublin Tune,
      with the Enterlud's

310 Mear, Tune, with the Enterlud's

311 Sonata

314 Shilli Ocary with Variations

318 The Stad Holders Minuet,
      with Variations

320 The Presidents Birth Night,
      with Variations

323 French Country Dance

324 Gavot, with Variation, by
      Mr. Handel

328 The Presidents March
      Coteree - Allegro

329 Buonaparts March [and] Quick-
      step

330 The Duke of Yorks March
      [and] Trio

331 Jefferson's March
      [and] Quick Step

333 The Dorsetshire March
      Clifton Spring

18. *MARYLAND: FREDERICK. MARSHALL L. ETCHISON COLLECTION (THOMAS SCHLEY 1)*

Page [Pagination supplied]   Page [Pagination supplied]

  409 Allegro, by Mr. Agrell   420 Marshal, Saxes Minuet
                                               Cotillion
  410 Guardian Angels

  411 Allegro by Pleyel   421 Holts Minuet
       With variations.   Fishers Hornpipe

  412 Lully's Minuet   422 Dubuorg's Minuet

  413 German Waltz   423 Giga by Sig'r Dubourg

  414 Caminianis Minuet   424 Sonata Allegro moderato
       Allamanda allegro by
          Corelli   425 Rondo

  416 Organ Piece, by Mr. Stanly -   INSIDE Hymn with Enterludes
       Slow andante, Trumpet stop BACK   Partly illegible.
                                COVER

  417 Giga by Leonard

  418 Solo for the Organ by Mr.
       Handel - Allegro moderato

  419 Giga by Corelli

19. *MARYLAND: FREDERICK. MARSHALL L. ETCHISON COLLECTION, C/O*
     MISS JOSEPHINE P. ETCHISON.

     "MUSIC FOR THE PIANA[SIC] FORTE: FAVORITE LESSONS
     FOR THE HARPSICHORD, OR, PIANO FORTE, COMPOSED,
     BY, THOMAS SCHLY." 168 [i.e., 173] pp. 10.5 x
     16 cm.

        Subtitle from alternate title-page (p. 3).

        Hand-sewn into embossed, orange-brown paper
        cover; title-page has ornamental border.

        Entries in same hand (same or similar to MS
        No. 18), except for pp. 50, 128-30, 136,
        146-49, which are possibly by the same but
        more hurried hand; same ink and paper.
        Pagination in the hand of the present
        owner.

        Inscriptions: "Thomas Schley," followed by six
        lines of Lorenzo's speech in Shakespeare's
        The Merchant of Venice (act 5, sc. 1) beginning,
        "The man that hath no music in himself...,"
        inside cover.

        The first two-thirds of the contents of this MS
        are generally included in MS No. 18; the last

third includes a variety of easy pieces.
This MS was not as carefully compiled as
No. 18, and there are a number of new pages
sewn over the originals, as well as erasures
and later, compressed additions. A. L.
Shifflet suggests that "its poorer condition,
as well as the nature of its contents, indicates
that this manuscript was much used, probably
for teaching purposes" ("Church Music and
Musical Life in Frederick, Maryland, 1745-1845,"
p. 16; for full citation and biographical notes
regarding Schley, see description of MS No.
18 above).

Page

Page

20. MASSACHUSETTS: BOSTON. BOSTON PUBLIC LIBRARY, MUSIC DIVISION.
     **M.129.124S; FORMERLY G.38.23.

SUPPLEMENT BOUND IN AN INCOMPLETE COPY OF THOMAS
WALTER'S GROUNDS AND RULES OF MUSICK (BOSTON: PRINTED
AND SOLD BY BENJAMIN MECOM, 1760). [18] pp. and
1 p. pasted inside back cover. 11.5 x 16.5 cm.

Bound in leather.

Inscriptions: "Amler Greenwood, Knoxville, Tenn.,
Nov., 1899," bookplate; "Wm. Cunningham, Esq.,

20. *MASSACHUSETTS: BOSTON. BOSTON PUBLIC LIBRARY (CUNNINGHAM-GREENWOOD)*

1765," "John Greenwood, 1835," "Chas. A. Greenwood, Detroit, Mich., 1870," appear among the MS hymns.

Some sacred hymns lacking from the printed edition are completed by MS hand closely imitating printed style; these are followed by popular airs, pp. [1]-[17], in a different hand.

This MS was described by Oscar Sonneck in his *Report on "The Star Spangled Banner," "Hail Columbia," "America," and "Yankee Doodle,"* p. 125. P. [10] below is reproduced there as Plate XIX. This is the earliest known MS version of the "Yankee Doodle" melody under the present title.

Melody only, unless otherwise indicated.

Page [Pagination supplied]

1 The Hero
   He comes, he comes, the
   hero comes
      For treble and bass; 2
      vv. as text, p. [4].

2 Lovely Nancy
   "Wrong." See also p.
   [13] below and inside
   back cover.
   The Blush

3 [Untitled]
   Treble and bass (incomplete); diamond notation.

4 [Blank]

5 Suky Bids Me
   A Trip to Halifax

6 God Save the King
   Chiling O Guiry

7 Trumpet Minuet

8 Prince Eugene's March

9 Bellisle March
   Mathew's Minuet

10 Yankey Doodle
   Sapphick Ode
   Footes Minuet

Page [Pagination supplied]

11 French Minuet

12 Lady Coventry's Minuet

13 Welcome Again
   Lovely Nancy
      See also p. [2] above
      and inside back cover.

14 Granoes March

15 Dorchester March
   Hesian Minuet

16 Reeds March
   The British Granadiers

17 Rural Felicity
   [Untitled hymn]
      How precious is the book
      divine

18 [Blank]

INSIDE   Lovely Nancy, with
BACK   Variations
COVER   See also pp. [2] and
             [13] above.

21. *MASSACHUSETTS: STURBRIDGE. OLD STURBRIDGE VILLAGE, RESEARCH LIBRARY, MANUSCRIPT DIVISION. 1971.34BV (MUSIC BOOK)*

"JOSEPH AKERMAN'S BOOK GIVEN HIM BY JOHN P. PAYSON, 1795." 81 p. 12.5 x 25 cm.

Bound in half-leather; marbled paper over boards. Lacking pp. 1-3.

Entries by different hands and inks; some later entries in pencil.

Inscriptions: "James P. Bartlett," p. 6; James P. Bartlett, 1826," p. 28; "Edward G. Bartlett," p. 16; "John Bartlett, Portsmouth, N. H.," p. 31; "Miss Sarah K. Bartlett," pp. 51, 52; "Thos. A. Adams," p. 51; "Debby Giles," p. 76; solmization exercise, in pencil, dated Feb. 1 (or 12?), 1836, written into inked lines by hand same as or similar to the first hand, p. 24.

Rudiments of singing, pp. 4-5. Flute gamut, with illustration of flute, p. 6. "Index," p. 6, but not entered. Hymns, one song text ("Indian Philosopher"), and 4 secular titles (in much later hand) in pencil, pp. 8-33.

Melody only, unless otherwise indicated.

Page

34 [Untitled]
      In pencil. Same melody
      as pp. 45, 50, and
      51 below.

35 A Highland Lad My Love Was
      Born

36 [Blank]

37 Blue Bells of Scotland
   The Last Beam is Shining
      See also p. 37 below.

38 [Untitled]
      Attempts to harmonize
      the preceding.

39 [Blank]

40 [Blank]

41 No. 1 English Lesson
      3 parts (only 2 copied).

42 No. 2 Major Minor
      3 parts (only 2 copied).

Page

43 Free Masons March
      3 parts (only 2 copied);
      the words "March" and
      "Connecticut" also writ-
      ten in.
   Pepprell March
      3 parts (only melody cop-
      ied); the word "Connec-
      ticut" also written in.
   Soft Be the Gently Breathing
   Notes
      Words only; music, p. 49
      below.

45 See Our Sail Well and Spray
      First five measures only.
      Same melody as pp. 34,
      50, and 51.

46 Cambridge
      Tenor only.

47 [Blank]

21. *MASSACHUSETTS: STURBRIDGE. OLD STURBRIDGE VILLAGE (JOSEPH AKERMAN)*

Page

48   Hark While Our Ship &c.
     Hark while our ship is
     springing
        V. 2 as text in later
        hand in pencil.

49   Soft Be the Gently Breathing
     Notes
     Soft be the gently
     breathing notes
        Vocal duet with keyboard;
        words as text, p. 44
        above.

50   The Wild Chase of Lutrow
     See our Oars with Feathered
     Spray
        Only part of melody
        copied. See also pp. 34,
        45, and 51.

51   See Our Oars with Feathered
     Spray
        4 parts. See also pp.
        34, 45, and 50 above.

52   [Blank]

53   New Mariners
     You gentlemen of England
     that live at home at ease
        3 parts; vv. 2-3 as
        text.

55   Blue Bonnets
        Much later hand; in
        pencil.

56   [Blank]

57   Roslin Castle
     Twas in that season of
     the year
        2 parts (only melody
        copied); vv. 2-4 as
        text.

59   Leson by Morelli
        3 parts (only treble and
        bass copied).

60   The Hermit
        Treble and bass (the bass
        incomplete).

Page

61   The Little Sailor Boy
     The sea was calm
        Vv. 2-3 as text.

62   Crazy Jane

63   Courtier's Think It No Harm
     London Ladies
     Irish Trot
     Lillibullero
     Tom Tinker's My True Love

65   Come Now All Ye Social Powers
     Come now all ye social
     powers
        Vv. 2-5 as text.

66   Gramachree Molly
     As down on bana's banks
     I stray'd
        Vv. 2-6 as text.

67   The Sailor's Epitaph
     Here a sheer hulk lies
     poor Tom Boling
        Vv. 2-3 as text.

68   How Blest Has My Time Been
     How blest has my time been
        Vv. 2-5 as text.

69   Nobody
     If to force me to sing it
     be your intention
        Vv. 2-7 as text.

70   Somebody
        Title only.

71   Tartan Pladdie
     British Grenadiers

72   Adams & Liberty
     Ye sons of Columbia
        Treble and bass, with
        introduction and postlude
        for keyboard.

73   Lady Berkly's Whim
     Chane[?] Cotillion
     The Maid in the Pump Room
     Jenny Sutton

74   Shay's March
     Hollow Drum

Page   Page

      Merry Dance   76 Debonnair
      The New Room   Chorus Jigg
75 Successful Compain   Boston March
      The Bower   77 York Fusileers
      Flowers of Edinburg   Mrs. Casey
      Cupid Recruiting Sargent   La belle Catherine

22. *MASSACHUSETTS: STURBRIDGE. OLD STURBRIDGE VILLAGE, RESEARCH LIBRARY, MANUSCRIPT DIVISION. 1968.45BV (MUSIC BOOK).*

"A COLECTION OF MUSIC IN TWO VOLUMES, COLLECTED BY JONATHAN SHIPLEY COPP; BEGUN IN THE MONTH OF JANUARY, 1799." 2 volumes in 1. 29 x 23 cm.

    Bound in half-leather; marbled paper over boards.

    Entries in same hand and on same kind of paper.

    Inscriptions: "Auctor nunc creditur esse mortuus et omnibus ____ [illegible] est in annum mille octo centi et tred__ [illegible] Domini Beltone Copp," title-page; see also p. 25 below.

    Profile vignettes of Washington and Franklin inside front cover; drawing of Edwin's Urn and house (1/2 p.) facing index; drawing of house facing back fly-leaf.

    Volume 1 contains 10 numbered pages of sacred melodies (without words), 14 blank leaves, and 4 pages of moral observations, followed by 6 blank leaves. Volume 2 contains 22 numbered pages, 3 unnumbered pages, 8 blank leaves, index, followed by 5 blank pages; includes songs with and without music, and moral observations.

    Listed below are the songs with music in volume 2.

Page   Page

1 Indian Chief   highest hill
    The sun sets at night and   Treble with bass; 4 vv.
    the stars shun the day   as text, followed by 2d
      Treble with bass;   part, The Answer, 4 vv.
      10 vv. as text.   as text.

3 Mary's Dream   4 Adams and Liberty
    The moon had climb'd the   Ye sons of Columbia who

22. *MASSACHUSETTS: STURBRIDGE. OLD STURBRIDGE VILLAGE (JONATHAN SHIPLEY COPP)*

Page

Page

bravely have fought
   Treble with bass; 9 vv.
   as text.

6 Disappointed Lover
   Tho youth and beauty grace
   the fair
      Treble with bass; 6 vv.
      as text.

8 Bunker's Hill
   Why should vain mortals
   3 parts; 15 vv.
      as text.

10 Emmanuel
   Behold as the shepherds
   were guarding their sheep
      Treble with bass; 6 vv.
      as text.

11 The Hermit
   At the close of the day
   when the hamlet was still
      Treble with bass; 6 vv.
      as text.

13 An Elegy on Sophronia
   Forbear my friends, forbear
      Treble with bass; 9 vv.
      as text.

16 Leander and Hero
   Leander on the bay of
   Hellespont
      Treble with bass; 6 vv.
      as text.

17 The Bee
   As Cupid in the garden
   stray'd
      Treble with bass; 4 vv.
      as text.

20 Primrose Hill
   On Primrose Hill there lived
   a lass
      Treble with bass; 7 vv.
      as text.

[25] Hymn Sung at N. London on the
   25th of June 1799 on the
   Occasion of Laying the
   Foundation Stone of Free
   Masons Hall.
   Thou great first cause
      Words only, but included
      here because of the date
      and event.

23. *MASSACHUSETTS: STURBRIDGE. OLD STURBRIDGE VILLAGE, RESEARCH LIBRARY, MANUSCRIPT DIVISION. 1962.59 (MUSIC BOOK).*

"JACOB LEONARD HIS BOOK. FEBRUARY 24, 1790."
[42] pp. and insert [4] pp. 10 x 19.5 cm.

Bound in paper covers.

Entries in same hand and ink but on different
kinds of paper; insert in different hand.

Contains 18 sacred, 4-part songs with words
and 1 song without words (on insert). The
final song is secular, and, according to
Sonneck-Upton (p. 311), was written by Jezaniah
Sumner (1754-1836) in 1798 on the occasion of
the first exhibition of the Bristol Academy,
Taunton, Mass. The secular song is listed below.

MASSACHUSETTS: STURBRIDGE. OLD STURBRIDGE VILLAGE ("THE BRITISH 25. HERO")

Page [Pagination supplied]

38-41 Ode on Science
          The morning sun shines from the east
             4 parts (only tenor and bass complete);
             counter-tenor not copied.

24. *MASSACHUSETTS: STURBRIDGE. OLD STURBRIDGE VILLAGE, RESEARCH LIBRARY, MANUSCRIPT DIVISION. 1963.40 (MUSIC BOOK).*

"A COLLECTION OF SONGS, &C. MARCH 18, 1814 [? YEAR CROSSED THROUGH]. 80 pp. 15.5 cm.

Bound in newspapers, apparently of Concord, N. H., bearing dates between May 27 and June 29, 1790.

Entries in same hand and ink and on same paper.

Inscriptions: none, but includes poem entitled "An Elegiac Ode Occasioned by the Early and Much Lamented Death of the Amiable Mrs. Lucy Loomis," pp. 9-14.

In addition to the songs with keyboard (treble and bass) listed below, the MS contains words to 22 other songs or poems, including Francis Hopkinson's "Battle of the Kegs (with indicated tune "Maggy Lawder")," pp. 36-39.

Page

27-29 A New Song, for a Serenade
          These, my Delia, heavenly charmer
             8 vv. as text.

55-56 [Untitled]
          I vow, I'll scream, don't think I'll feign
             3 vv. as text.

Page

59-61 God Save America
          God save America
             4 vv. as text.

62-67 British Grenadier
          Fair Britain's boast no longer
             Treble only; 12 vv. as text.

80 Vicar and Moses

25. *MASSACHUSETTS: STURBRIDGE. OLD STURBRIDGE VILLAGE, RESEARCH LIBRARY, MANUSCRIPT DIVISION. 1968.43 (MUSIC BOOK).*

COMMONPLACE BOOK. [50] pp. 9.5 x 15.5 cm.

Rough-sewn into paper covers in 2 uneven signatures. Lacking pp. [41]-[44].

25. *MASSACHUSETTS: STURBRIDGE. OLD STURBRIDGE VILLAGE. ("THE BRITISH HERO")*

Entries in same hand but in different inks.

Inscriptions: "Northfield," title-page; memoranda in different hand dated 1776-86 included on final pages.

Includes rudiments for singing.

All titles are sacred except the one listed below.

Page [Pagination supplied]

27 The British Hero
He comes, he comes, the hero comes
2 parts (tenor and bass); in diamond notation;
2 vv. as text.

26. *MASSACHUSETTS: STURBRIDGE. OLD STURBRIDGE VILLAGE, RESEARCH LIBRARY, MANUSCRIPT DIVISION. 1964.63 (MUSIC BOOK).*
"ELEGY ON SOPHRONIA." [2] pp. 33cm.

Single sheet, music copied on p. [1] only.

Inscription: "Durham, Sept. 19, 1800," p. [1].

For SATB (melody in tenor); text, 12 vv., on both sides of sheet.

First line: Forbear, my friends, forbear, and ask no more

27. *MASSACHUSETTS: WORCESTER. AMERICAN ANTIQUARIAN SOCIETY. [NO SHELF NUMBER]*
COMMONPLACE BOOK. 1-155 [i.e., 157] pp. 10 x 16 cm.

Bound in leather. Lacking pp. 1-13, 30-33, 54-55, 151-153; pp. 80-81 partially torn; p. 145 numbered twice.

Entries possibly in same hand and ink and on same paper.

"Instructions for Clarionette," inside front cover. Index, last page.

Chiefly hymns; "Devotion," p. 131, attributed to

D. Read, 1810, and "China," p. 132, attributed
to T. Swan, 1801, in later hand. Only secular
titles are listed below.

Melody only, unless otherwise indicated.

Page		Page	
14	March in *The God of Love* Yankey Doodle	22	[3] Lesson[s]
15	Washington's March	23	Belleisle March Boston March
16	Marquis of Granby's March 　　3 parts. Freemasons March	24	For There's No Luck About 　　the House Dog and Gun Canada Farewell
17	Durham March Prince Eugene's March	25	Wood Cutters Love's March
18	Duke of Holstein's March March to Boston	26	London March
19	Lesson by Morelli	27	Favorite Air Air in *Rosina*
20	March in The Battle of Prague Turkish March	28	Col. Orne's March
		29	The Pantheon

28. *MASSACHUSETTS: WORCESTER. AMERICAN ANTIQUARIAN SOCIETY. [NO
SHELF NUMBER]*

SINGLE SHEET FROM UNIDENTIFIED COLLECTION.
[2] pp. 4.5 x 22.5 cm.

Possibly copied from editions published in
New Haven, 1786, cf. Sonneck-Upton, pp.
350, 374.

Page [Pagination supplied]	Page [Pagination supplied]
[1]　Queen Mary's Lamentation 　　I sigh and lament in vain 　　Treble and bass; words 　　for 1 v. underlain.	[2]　[Untitled] 　　The heavy hours are almost 　　past 　　　Keyboard figuration 　　　without melody; incomplete.

29. *MICHIGAN: ANN ARBOR. UNIVERSITY OF MICHIGAN, WILLIAM L. CLEMENTS
LIBRARY. ANDREW LAW PAPERS: MS MUSIC: SECULAR SONGS (ACCESSION
NO. MS 61-2507).*

"SONG, SUNG BY MR. BAKER." [2] pp. 30 cm.

29. *MICHIGAN: ANN ARBOR. UNIVERSITY OF MICHIGAN. (MR. BAKER'S SONG)*

Single sheet, music copied on both sides.

Although included in Andrew Law's papers, probably not in his hand.

Melody and figured bass; includes instrumental introduction and interludes.

First line: Who upon the oozy beach

30. *MICHIGAN: ANN ARBOR. UNIVERSITY OF MICHIGAN, WILLIAM L. CLEMENTS LIBRARY, MANUSCRIPTS DIVISION: HOOKE.*

MUSIC COPIED AT BACK OF JOURNAL OF GEORGE PHILIP HOOKE, 1780. 2 leaves, [vi, 48] pp. 12 x 19.5 cm.

Bound in one-quarter brown leather (deteriorated) over brown boards.

Inscriptions: "Orderly Book, 17th Infantry [crossed through] Grs. G. P. Hooke," inside front cover; "Major Hooke," inside back cover.

George Philip Hooke, officer of the first battalion of Grenadiers of the British Army, described the voyage from New York to South Carolina and the siege of Charlestown in this journal. Includes 27 catches, probably copied from collections of catches by Harrington, Hayes, and Purcell published in London, ca. 1780. The music was apparently not published in America before 1800.

Index, p. [i]-[ii], lists 30 items, of which Nos. 20-22 are lacking.

For 3 or 4 voices, in treble clefs; each entry is numbered both in Index and in place. Music copied from back cover.

Page [Pagination supplied]		Page [Pagination supplied]	
1	1. The Quakers Wedding, a Catch for Three Voices. Slow Sister! Sister!	5	3. A Laughing Catch by Mr. Harrington, for Three Voices I cannot sing this catch 4 staves.
3	2. The Assignation, a Catch for Three Voices by Mr. Harrington. Not too fast Come where shall we walk	7	4. Catch, for Three Voices, by Mr. H. Purcell Jack thou'rt a toper 4 staves.

Page [Pagination supplied]

9 5. Catch, for 4 Voices, by
      Mr. H. Purcell
      Soldier Soldier

10 6. A Favorite Catch, by Dr.
      Hayes, for 3 Voices.
      Affetoso.
      Haste ye soft gales
      4 staves.

11 7. Isabel, a Catch for Three
      Voices
      Ye sweet gliding streems

13 8. A Catch for 3 Voices.
      Larghetto
      Oh that I had wings like
      a dove

15 9. A Yawning Catch, to Affect
      the Company with, for
      3 Voices, by Mr.
      Harrington
      'Tis Hum-drum

17 10. A Catch, for 3 Voices,
      by Mr. Harrington
      Give me the sweet de-
      lights of love
      4 staves.

19 11. Love and Musick, a
      Favorite Catch for 3
      Voices, by Mr.
      Harrington
      How great is the pleasure

21 12. A Catch, for 3 Voices:
      Come Honest Friends
      Come honest friends

23 13. There Stands the Wife of
      Jealous Roger, a Catch
      for 3 Voices. Moderato
      There stands the wife

27 14. A Catch for 4 Voices:
      Don't Push Your
      Tender Passion
      Dont, dont, dont push
      The word "Passion" ex-
      tends to p. [28] in the
      title.

Page [Pagination supplied]

28 15. Catch for 4 Voices:
      A Fig for Care
      A fig for care

29 16. I Faint I Die, a Catch
      for 4 Voices
      I faint I die

30 17. Nose, Nose: Catch for
      4 Voices
      Nose, Nose, Nose, Nose

31 18. Chloe Yeild'd on the
      Morrow Sighing: Catch
      for 3 Voices
      Chloe, Chloe yeild'd

33 19. Wou'd You Sing a Catch w.
      Pleasure, for 3 Voices
      Woud you sing a catch

   *20. Hott Mutton Pies Hott
   *21. When Is It Best Said John
      to Joan
   *22. Care the Canker of Our Joys

35 23. Glee by Mr. Purcell, for 3
      Voices. Grazzioso
      Fairest isle of isles

39 24. Catch for 3 Voices
      White sand and grey sand

40 25. Look Neighbours Look:
      Catch for 3 Voices
      Look neighbours

41 26. Joan Said to John: Catch
      for 3 Voices
      Joan said to John

43 27. Mr. Speaker Tho 'Tis Late:
      Catch for 3 Voices
      Mr. Speaker tho 'tis late

46 28. O Beautious Eyes Discover:
      Catch for 3 Voices
      O beautious eyes

47 29. Half an Hour past 12 O'Clock:
      Catch for 4 Voices
      Half an hour

48 30. Oh Absalom My Son: Catch for
      3 Voices
      Oh Absalom my son

*These items are now missing; titles supplied from index.

31. MICHIGAN: FLINT. BLY CORNING (PRIVATE COLLECTION).

"SAMMLUNG ERBAULICHER LIEDER [COLLECTION OF
EDIFYING SONGS]." [34] pp., [11] leaves.
35 cm.

Cover title.

Hand-sewn into thick paper wrappers; last
3 leaves mutilated.

Entries in various hands, in ink, and on same
kind of paper.

Inscription: "*Pennsylvania Packet* (Philadelphia),
August 24th, 1790," p. [20].

In addition to the music listed below, there are
texts of 16 other melodies, chiefly English and
German drinking songs, in part with staves drawn
and tempo indications given.

Melody only, in treble clef; words all copied
as text.

Page [Pagination supplied]

1 Toby reduc'd. Lively
   Dear Tom this brown jug
   that now foams with
   mild ale
     3 vv.

3 A Humorous Song. Allegro
     moderato
   The prigs who are troubled
   with consciences qualms
     3 vv.

5 Contentment
   No glory I covet, no
   riches I want
     5 vv.

7 The Echoeing Horn
   The echoeing horn call's
   the sportsmen abroad
     2 vv.

9 Bustle and Stir in My Shop
   In choice of a husband
   we widows are nice
     3 vv.; "sung by Mrs.
   Heaphy" noted following
   the last verse.

Page [Pagination supplied]

11 The Mistress
    What e'er squeamish lovers
    may say
      5 vv.

13 How Happy a State Does a
      Miller Possess
    How happy a state does
    a miller possess
      3 vv.

15 [Untitled]
    Alles kommt zu seinem Ende
      4 vv., in German script;
      note in upper right cor-
      ner, partially lacking
      due to mutilation: "Chanté
      par Sa..."

18 The Triumph of Love, the words
      by Captn. Morris
    Tho Bacchus may boast of
    his care-killing bowl
      3 vv.

31 [Untitled]
    Bekränzt mit Laub den
    liebvollen Becher
      8 vv., in German script.

Page [Pagination supplied]   Page [Pagination supplied]

33 [Untitled]   34 The Mutt
                                       Let others boast the
                                       downy nest
                                       4 vv.

*32. NEW YORK: ALBANY. NEW YORK STATE LIBRARY, MANUSCRIPT AND
HISTORY LIBRARY. ACCESSION NO. 15087.*

COMMONPLACE BOOK. [54] pp. 17 x 25.5 cm.

Unbound; rough-sewn.

Different, less tutored hand begins p. [21];
same kind of ink and paper.

Inscription: "March 29, 1791," p. [16].

For voice and keyboard (treble and bass with
chords usually only at cadences), or keyboard
alone (treble and bass), unless otherwise
indicated.

Page [Pagination supplied]   Page [Pagination supplied]

1 The Topsails   12 Mary's Dream
     The topsails shivers in   The moon had climbed the
     the wind   highest hill
        See also p. [51]   For one or two voices
        below.   and keyboard; vv.
                                           2-4 as text.
2 Anna's Urn
                                  14 Rose Tree
3 Minuetto   A rose tree in full bearing
   Rural Felicity   V. 2 as text.

4 Moderato par Foose   15 Chorus by Rolle, Adapted for
     When the rosy morn appearing   the Piano Forte
                                        Praise the Lord, praise
5 My Dog and My Gun   the Lord, for on us shineth
                                           For one or two voices
6 [Untitled]   and keyboard.
     Bright Phoebus has mounted
     the chariot of day   16 Ma chere amie
        See also p. [24] below.   Ma chere amie, my charming
                                        fair
8 [Untitled]
     Unto us a Child is born   17 Guardian Angels
                                        Guardian angels now pro-
9 Stern's Maria   tect me
     Twas near a thicket's
     calm retreat   18 Allamon
        Vv. 2-3 as text.   Fingering inscribed.

11 Roseline Castle

32. *NEW YORK: ALBANY.   NEW YORK STATE LIBRARY (ANON.)*

Page [Pagination supplied] Page [Pagination supllied]

Good Morrow to your Night
  Cap
  Fingering inscribed.

19 Allamando
  Fingering inscribed.

20 Lass of Aberdeen
  Incomplete.
  Slings Beas [i.e., Slingsby's]
  Allaman, or Dall fresque
  [with] Trio

21 Malbrouck
  The Banks of Banna

22 The Turks March
  Lovely Nymph

23 Gramachree

24 Bright Phoebus
  Bright Phoebus has mounted
  his chariot of day
  See also p. [6] above.

28 The Primrose Girl
  Come buy of poor Kate

30 Bonny Jem of Aberdeen
  The tuneful lavrocks cheer
  the grove

32 Script, or Surprize

33 Rondo

34 Pauvre Madelon
  Could you to battle march
  away

36 The Twins of Latona

40 When William at Eve
  When William at eve

42 Rondo

43 Contredance

44 The Tear
  My heart from my bosom
  would fly
  Vv. 2-3 as text.

46 Allegro

47 Washington Resigned

48 The Wedding Day
  What virgin or shepherd

51 The Topsail
  The topsailes shiver in
  the wind
  See also p. [1] above.

52 [Untitled]
  O'er barren hills and flowr'y
  dales

54 Lady Coventry's Minuett
  Green Fields

33. *NEW YORK: BROOKLYN.   MRS. ALMA DRAKE (PRIVATE COLLECTION).*

SINGLE SHEET CONTAINING WORKS BY FRANCIS
HOPKINSON. [2] pp. 33.5 cm.

Inscriptions: "Fra Hopkinson [signature],"
p. [1]; Hopkinson's signature also on p. [2].

Formerly in the collection of Carl Tollefsen,
whose article in the *Musical Courier* contains
a facsimile reproduction of the first work.
Oscar Sonneck, in his *Francis Hopkinson and James
Lyon*, reproduces the first work from an earlier
MS (opposite p. 31), and gives considerable
detail about both works in Chapter 4.

Page

Page

[1 Untitled]
 My days have been so
 wondrous free &c.
  For voice and keyboard,
  with keyboard introduc-
  tion, interlude, and
  epilogue.

[2] Washington's March, as Per-
  formed at the New Theatre,
  Philadelphia, 1791.
  For keyboard.

*34. NEW YORK: NEW YORK CITY. COLUMBIA UNIVERSITY LIBRARIES, DIV-
ISION OF SPECIAL COLLECTIONS, RARE BOOK AND MANUSCRIPT
LIBRARY. SPEC. MS. COLL.: HUNT-BEROL: BROADHURST, MISS D.,
SELECTIONS FROM OPERATIC ROLES.*

COPYBOOK CONTAINING WORDS AND MUSIC OF SOPRANO
ROLES IN SEVEN OPERAS SUNG BY MISS D. BROADHURST.
1 leaf, [175] pp., 1 leaf. 23 x 30 cm.

Bound in half-leather; marbled paper over
boards.

Entries in different hands (the 1st, 5th, and
6th works below possibly in the hand of
Benjamin Carr) and in different inks.

Inscriptions: "D. Broadhurst" and "No. 180,"
the latter in the hand of Benjamin Carr,
inside front cover (for MSS similarly numbered
in Carr's hand, see Nos. 35, 54, 62, 64, and 65);
"Carr & Schetky," p. [1].

Miss Broadhurst, of the Covent Garden Opera
in England, emigrated to Philadelphia in 1793,
moved to Boston in 1797, and died in Charleston,
S. C., according to John R. Parker in his
Musical Biography, pp. 186-89. She is known to
have been a leading operatic soprano of the period.
J. George Schetky joined Benjamin Carr in his
publishing company in Philadelphia soon after
1800.

Table of Contents, inside front cover.

The first seven titles below are operas, each
consisting of arias, recitatives, duets, etc.,
for voice(s) and keyboard, in part with added
instrumentation indicated; the last two titles
are separate works.

34. NEW YORK: NEW YORK CITY. COLUMBIA UNIVERSITY (D. BROADHURST)

Page	[Pagination supplied]	Page	[Pagination supplied]
1	*Double Disguise*	162	[Blank]
22	[Blank]	163	*The Waterman*
23	*Thomas and Sally*	167	St. Andrew's Day
56	[Blank]		A cruel fate hangs threatening
57	*Two Misers*		Glee (SATB); vv. 2-3 as text.
108	[Blank]	172	[Blank]
109	*Elfrida*	173	[Blank]
146	[Blank]	174	[Untitled]
147	*Lionel and Clarissa*		Love's a joy fraught with sorrow
158	[Blank]		For voice and keyboard.
159	*Love in a Village*		

35. NEW YORK: NEW YORK CITY. COLUMBIA UNIVERSITY LIBRARIES, DIV-
ISION OF SPECIAL COLLECTIONS, RARE BOOK AND MANUSCRIPT LIBRARY.
SPEC. MS. COLL.: HUNT-BEROL: BENJAMIN CARR, MS. NOTEBOOK,
CA. 1793.

COPYBOOK COMPILED BY BENJAMIN CARR CONTAINING
SONGS, ARIAS, ETC.   [84] pp. 24.5 x 37 cm.

Entries in Carr's hand, pp. [1]-[61]; pp.
[66]-[84] are in a different hand, opening
from the back and proceeding toward the center.

Inscriptions: "Benjn. Carr [signature]" and
"No. 159," title-page; "B. Carr, 17 Nov., 1793,"
p. [49]; "Carr," p. [51]. For MSS similarly
numbered in Carr's hand, see Nos. 34, 54, 62, 64,
and 65.

Only entries pp. [1]-[61] are listed below; pp.
[66]-[84] consist of excerpts from *Judas Maccabeus, Theodora, L'Allegro ed il pensieroso,* and *Joshua,*
by Händel.

For voice and keyboard, unless otherwise noted;
titles in brackets supplied from Sonneck-Upton
(pp. [10], [14], [20], [24], [42], [56]) or
Wolfe (pp. [4], [6], [12], [18]).

Page	[Pagination supplied]	Page	[Pagination supplied]
1	[The Wolf, by] Shield	2	[Untitled]
	At the **peaceful** midnight hour		Gates are barr'd a vain resistance

Page [Pagination supplied]

Page [Pagination supplied]

4   [Queen Mary's Lamentation,
        by] Giordani
        I sigh & lament me in vain

6   [With Lowly Suit, from *No
        Song, No Supper,* by]
        Storace
        My native land I bade adieu
        See also p. [10] below.

8   [Untitled, by] Dr. Hayes
        To thy cliffs rocky Seaton
        adieu

10 [My Native Land, from *The
        Haunted Tower,* by] Storace
        My native land I bade adieu
        See also p. [6] above.

12 [Black-eyed Susan, by]
        Leveridge
        All in the downs the fleet
        was moor'd
        Melody only.

14 [Forever Fortune]
        Forever fortune wilt thou
        prove

16 [Untitled, by] Shield
        Charming Clorinda evry
        note you breathe

18 [What Wakes This New Pain,
        by] Linley
        What wakes this new pain in
        my breast

20 [Ere around the Huge Oak,
        from *The Farmer,* by] Shield
        Ere around the huge oak

22 [Untitled]
        Perhaps it is not love
        said I

24 [The Indigent Peasant, by]
        Hook
        Tho the muses neer smile by
        the light of the sun

26 [Untitled, by] Paisiello
        Sutto dai voi dipenda tutto
        tentar vilice

29 What Citadel So Proud Can Say,
        [by] Arnold
        What citadel so proud can
        say

31 The Match Girl
        Come buy of poure Mary

32 [Untitled, by Handel] Sung by
        Sigra Cuzzoni in *Admetus*
        Jo ti bacio o bella unviage

33 The Soldiers Last Retreat
        Alas the battals lost
        and won

35 Poor Peg, [by] Dibdin
        Poor Peggy lov'd a soldier
        lad

38 The Sailor's Return
        Bleak was the morn

42 [The Sailor Boy, by Storace]
        Poll dang' it how d'ye do

44 Captivity, a Ballad Supposed
        to be Sung by the Unfor-
        tunate Marie Antoinette
        during Her Confinement,
        composed by S Horace [i.e.,
        Storace]
        My foes prevail, my friends
        are fled
        Incomplete.

46 Ballad from Shakespear[e's
        Measure for Measure, by
        Carr]
        Tell me where is fancy bred
        Melody only. Published
        by Carr in 1794; see
        Sonneck-Upton, p. 424.

50 [Untitled, from Shakespeare's
        Love's Labour Lost, by
        Carr]
        When icicles hang by the wall
        Published by Carr in 1794;
        see Sonneck-Upton, p. 462.

52 [Untitled]
        I die, O take those lips away

35. *NEW YORK: NEW YORK CITY. COLUMBIA UNIVERSITY (BENJAMIN CARR, COPYBOOK)*

Page [Pagination supplied]   Page [Pagination supplied]

   54 For 2 Patent Flutes with   58 [Untitled]
          Additional Reg[ister]   Oh! tell me softly breathing
                                                gale
   56 [Poor Black Boy]
         Your care of money, ah   62 [Blank]
         care naw more
                                          63 [Blank]

                                          64 [Blank]

                                          65 [Blank]

36. *NEW YORK: NEW YORK CITY. COLUMBIA UNIVERSITY LIBRARIES, DIV-*
    ISION OF SPECIAL COLLECTIONS, RARE BOOK AND MANUSCRIPT LIBRARY.
    SPEC. MS. COLL.: HUNT-BEROL: CARR, BENJAMIN, COLLECTION OF VOCAL
    SCORES: "DELIA FAIR," CARR MS. SONG.

   "DELIA FAIR." [2] pp. 33 cm.

   Single sheet, music copied on both sides.

   Believed to be by Benjamin Carr, but apparently
   not published. The MS is included in a volume
   of sheet music printed in England. The name,
   "B. Carr," is handwritten at the beginning of
   the volume, and the back cover and fly-leaf
   have a list, in Carr's hand, of compositions,
   names of performers, and places of performances
   (incomplete), as well as other information.

   Treble and bass, with keyboard introduction
   and ritornello; words for vv. 2-4 cut from a
   printed volume and pasted on p. [2].

   First line: Swell the song in strain sublime

37. *NEW YORK: NEW YORK CITY. COLUMBIA UNIVERSITY LIBRARIES, DIV-*
    ISION OF SPECIAL COLLECTIONS, RARE BOOK AND MANUSCRIPT LIBRARY.
    X780.973 C68.

   "A COLLECTION OF DANCING TUNES, MARCHES, & SONG
   TUNES." [1] leaf, [58] pp. 13 x 17.5 cm.

   Bound in leather; end-papers of Boston newspapers
   bearing latest date of April 5, 1788.

   Entries in same hand and ink and on same paper.

   Inscription: "Whittier Perkins's book, 1790,"

on fly-leaf, (the MS is generally known by
this title).

This collection was described by Oscar Sonneck
in his   *Report on "The Star-Spangled Banner," "Hail
Columbia," "America" and Yankee Doodle,"* p. 124, and
p. [1] below is reproduced there as plate XVIII.
Columbia University announced in the *New York
Times* of Dec. 19, 1965 (section 1, p. 70) that the
collection apparently contained the earliest
recorded manuscript of "Yankee Doodle," dating
this commonplace book as 1777 or 1778. Sonneck's
earlier research, however, dated this version as
"about 1790" and dated another manuscript version
as "about 1780" (see MS No. 20 above).

For a treble melody instrument, probably flute;
this MS shares a common repertoire with the Henry
Beck flute book (MS No. 5 above), and a repertory
somewhat similar to John Carroll's violin book
(MS No. 14 above).

Melody only, unless otherwise indicated.

Page [Pagination supplied]

Page [Pagination supplied]

1 The Seven Stars
   Yankey Doodle
   The Haymakers Dance in
      Fortunatus
   Marble Hall in *The Genii*
   Charming Fair
   To Arms

2 Welcome Here Again
      Two versions.
   The Ladies Breast Knot
   Granleys Delight
   The Settee in *Queen Mab*

3 Pady Wack
   Farewell to Wives and
      Sweethearts
   The Polonese Dance in
      Perseus and Andromeda
   Pretty Cupid

4 The Hessian Camp
   Barley Sugar
   The Queen of Hearts
   The Feastwell [followed by,
      in a different hand,]
      A Quickstep
   Sukey Bids Me

5 The Dorsetshire March
   Mr. Buches Humeur
   There Was a Jolly Miller
   St. Patrick's Day in
      That Morning

6 The Mariners of Wicklow
   The Brick Maker
   General Wolf's March
   The New Negro

7 The Yellow Hair'd Laddie
      [with] Variations
   The Bonniest Lass in a'
      the World
   Street Her Up and Had Her
      Gaun

8 Success to the Fleet
   Thompson's Quick Step
   Jenny Nettle
   Lady Jane Stuarts Reel
   The Men to Make a Reel

9 Black Marys
   New Hob Nob
   Basket of Oisters

37. *NEW YORK: NEW YORK CITY. COLUMBIA UNIVERSITY (WHITTIER PERKINS)*

Page [Pagination supplied]   Page [Pagination supplied]

   A Tune to Chevy-Chase   54 The Lovers Recantation
   A Reel
   Reel   55 [Untitled]
   Reel   As Celia was learning on
   Reel   a spinnet to play
                                          2- or 3-part catch.
48 Damon & Clora
      Go false Damon   56 Sweet William & Susan
      Soprano and tenor.   Jockey to the Fair
                                          See also p. [28] above.
51 The Contented Swain
      Tenor and bass.   57 Johnny & Sally
   Woe to me   Says Johnny to Sally
                                         4 vv. as text.
52 Fire on the Mountains.
      A Reel   58 The Dauphin
   A Sweet Country Life   The Storm
   The Irish Girl   The General Toast
      Two versions.   The Storm
   The British Grenadiers   Variant of the preceding,
                                        last 8 measures only.
53 Washin[g]tons Health
      Here's Washingtons health
      & it shall go round
         Duet for tenor and bass.
   A Prison Song, or The
      Contented Prisoner

38. *NEW YORK: NEW YORK CITY. COLUMBIA UNIVERSITY LIBRARIES, DIV-
     ISION OF SPECIAL COLLECTIONS, RARE BOOK AND MANUSCRIPT LIBRARY.
     SPEC. MS. COLL.: HUNT-BEROL: THE FIRST ASSEMBLY. PHILADELPHIA.
     1783.*

     SINGLE SHEET CONTAINING DANCE MUSIC.   [2] pp.
     18.5 x 22.5 cm.

        Entries in same hand and ink.

        Inscription: "Philadelphia, 1783," p. [1].

        Melody only.

Page   Page

[1] The First Assembly   [2] [Untitled]
       Includes dance figures   [Untitled]
       below melody.

39. *NEW YORK: NEW YORK CITY. COLUMBIA UNIVERSITY LIBRARIES, DIV-*
ISION OF SPECIAL COLLECTIONS, RARE BOOK AND MANUSCRIPT LIBRARY.
SPEC. MS. COLL.: HUNT-BEROL: TO THE MEMORY OF WASHINGTON.

"TO THE MEMORY OF WASHINGTON." [4] pp. 33.5 cm.

Folded sheet, music copied on pp. [2]-[4];
p. [1] blank.

Entries in same hand and ink.

Contains two different tunes for the same
text: the first is for two voices, and the
second consists only of the melody.

First line: Immortal Chief

40. *NEW YORK: NEW YORK CITY. COLUMBIA UNIVERSITY LIBRARIES, DIV-*
ISION OF SPECIAL COLLECTIONS, RARE BOOK AND MANUSCRIPT LIBRARY.
SPEC. MS. COLL.: HUNT-BEROL: WHAT CARE I HOW FAIR SHE BE.

FOLDED SHEET CONTAINING 4 SONGS. [4] pp. 41.5 cm.

Entries in same hand but different ink.

Melody only; includes additional vv. of text
for last 3 songs, p. [2].

Page [Pagination supplied]

1 What Care I How Fair She Be
     Shall I, wasting in
     despair
        Vv. 2-3 as text.
   [Untitled]
     When first I ken'd young
     Sandies face

2 [Text; see description
     above]

Page [Pagination supplied]

3 The Soldiers Grave
     Of all sensation pity brings
   [Untitled]
     Hey for a lass and a bottle
     to cheer

4 [Blank]

41. *NEW YORK: NEW YORK CITY. JAMES J. FULD (PRIVATE COLLECTION)*

"MISS SUSAN ASSHETON'S BOOK. JANUARY 20TH
A DI. 1789." 135 pp. 13 x 21 cm.

Bound in brown leather over boards.

Entries nearly all in same hand and ink and
on same paper.

Miss Assheton, of Philadelphia, was born in
1767 and died in 1834; see the *Pennsylvania*

41. *NEW YORK: NEW YORK CITY. JAMES J. FULD (SUSAN ASSHETON)*

Magazine 55(April, 1931):174 and *Publications of the Geneological Society of Pennsylvania* 8(March, 1921):27, respectively. This commonplace book is described in Charles Hamilton's *Auction* [Catalog] no. 17 (February 1, 1967):72, item 241.

The MS was apparently copied over a period of several years, at least from 1789 (title-page) to 1814, the year of the siege of Fort McHenry. (The song-text, "O say can you see," occurs on pp. 80-82 under the title, "Fort McHenry;" it was first published with the music under the title, "The Star Spangled Banner," in 1814.)

Several pages were removed before the present sequential numbering in pencil. The MS, however, reads from two directions toward the center. The first fifteen songs in the backward direction are so numbered (with a few insertions; also the first three numbers are now bound out of order). These songs would appear to be the earliest in the collection, although the compiler may have initially reserved this direction for the melodies with words and the other direction for those without, and copied simultaneously in both.

Index (containing only one entry), p. 135.

Melody only, unless otherwise indicated.

Page		Page	
1	[Title-page]		The Hay-makers Dance
2	[Blank]	10	The Serenade
3	French Minuet		Master Tommy's Married
	For keyboard?	11	The Dusky Night
	Includes final chords.	12	The Social Pow'rs
4	Cotillion	13	How Imperfect
	Minuet		
5	Miss Ford's Dance	14	A Toast
	Lady Coventry's Minuet	15	Anna
6	He Comes	16	Colan
	When First I Saw the	17	The Rose
	Gracefull Move		See also p. 100 below.
7	All around the Maypole	19	Song from *The Deserter*
	Country Dance	20	Jockey
8	Prudence	21	La petit ballet
9	When Wars Alarms		

Here it is necessary to turn the book upside down and read from the opposite cover.

Page

Page

  91 [Songs without music]   84 [Blank]

  87 [Blank]   83 [Blank]

  86 Salvation   82 [Song without music; see
         Title in pencil, erased;   descriptive notes above
         treble & bass.   regarding Ft. McHenry]

42. NEW YORK: NEW YORK CITY.   JAMES J. FULD (PRIVATE COLLECTION).

"PHILO LEEDS, HIS BOOK. ANNADOMINY 1733."
[28] pp. 20 cm.

Hand-sewn; last page mutilated.

Entries in one or two hands [see below: the hands of father and son are indistinguishable], in same ink and paper.

Inscriptions: maxims and "Philo Leeds Jun. [signature]," title-page; "Philo Leeds Jun: His Book , Anno Do. 1734," p. [27]; maxims signed "Elizabeth Huff, 1795," p. [26]; "Joseph Leeds, his hand and pen, 1770," p. [28].

Philo Leeds was baptized August 27, 1702 or 3, and in 1719 lived in Northampton, N. J.; Philo Jun. was the younger of his two sons; see the New York Geneological and Biographical Society's *Register of Pedigrees* 2(1929):43, and C. L. Humeston's *Leeds: A New Jersey Family* (Philadelphia: B. F. Leeds, n.d.), pp. 4-5.

An Introduction to All Lovers of Psalmody (i.e., rudiments for singing), pp. [3]-[9]. For the Flute (i.e. rudiments), pp. [15]-[17]. The second group of rudiments may have been copied from *The Flute Master Compleat Improv'd ... Book the First* (1706), pp. 2-4. MS includes one secular title, listed below.

Melody only.

Page [Pagination supplied]

  21 [Untitled]
        Tentatively identified as a variant of "Katharine Ogie"; printed in Music Library Association *Notes* 34(1977):504.

43. *NEW YORK: NEW YORK CITY. JAMES J. FULD (PRIVATE COLLECTION).*

"A GOOD SELECTION OF MARCHES AND OTHER PIECES."
35 pp.   9.5 x 16 cm.

Bound in blue cardboard with paper spine.

Entries probably in same hand and ink and on same paper.

Inscription: "James Pike [signature]," title-page (this is presumably the Rev. James Pike (1703-1792) of Somersworth, N. H., among whose papers this MS was found).

Melody only, unless otherwise indicated.

Page [Even-numbered pages blank]   Page [Even-numbered pages blank]

1	[Title-page]
3	Bold Highlander
	Drops of Brandy
5	White Cockade. C. T. March
	The Seven Stars, a Double Dragg
	On the Way to the Field
7	Successful Campaign
	Handel's March. C. T.
	To Arms
	Drummer's Call
9	Cupid's March
	Father Knows His Own House
11	Boston March
	Baltimore, a March
13	The Three Cheers
	French Grenadiers March or Salute
	Scotch Favorite
15	Rogue's March
	On the Way to Boston
	The Troop
	Fifer's Master-piece

17	The Marionets Cotillion, a March
	Sophronia. An Elegy on Sophronia, Who Died of the Small-Pox, 1711. [By?] King
	For SATB (melody in tenor).
19	Hartland
	Freemason's March
	Yankey Doodle
21	Irish Washerwoman
	Jockey to the Fair
23	[Blank]
25	[Blank]
27	Spring. L. M. [By?] Smith
	Gently he draws my heart along
	For STB (melody in tenor).
29	[Blank staves]
31	[Blank staves]
33	[Blank staves]
35	[Blank]

44. *NEW YORK: NEW YORK CITY. JAMES J. FULD (PRIVATE COLLECTION).*

COMMONPLACE BOOK CONTAINING POEMS, PROSE, HYMNS, SONG-TEXTS, ETC.   [46] leaves.   10 x 16.5 cm.

Paper covers roughly sewn into leather spine.

Entries in several hands and inks.

Inscriptions: many different names on both fly-leaves; earliest date, March 27, 1779, on back fly-leaf; latest date cited within the MS, July 4, 1822.

No music. This MS is mentioned solely because it contains a copy of the song-text, "The Yankee's Return from Camp" (i.e., "Yankee Doodle"), leaves [24*v*]-[25*r*]. The text (14 verses) is essentially the same as that of the broadsides illustrated in Plates XXI-XXIII of Oscar Sonneck's *Report on "The Star-Spangled Banner," "Hail Columbia," "America," and "Yankee Doodle"* and described there on pp. 138-42. Sonneck assigns dates to these broadsides between 1775 and 1813 or later.

45. *NEW YORK: NEW YORK CITY.   NEW YORK HISTORICAL SOCIETY.   MANU-SCRIPTS: MUSIC: B.V. SEC.: GREENWOOD, JOHN.*

COMMONPLACE BOOK CONTAINING FLUTE MUSIC, OWNED BY JOHN GREENWOOD. [1] leaf, 87 leaves, [1] leaf. 15.5 x 20 cm.

Bound in original leather, partially repaired, over paper; front cover bears legend concerning Greenwood's army service. Lacking leaves 76-77, 82-86.

Entries in same hand and ink, except leaves 60, 73, 79, 80*r* and one loose-leaf insert, dated London, August 26th, 1831. "Rough Sketch of the Watermark of This Paper," pasted over leaf 81 , is dated June 15, 1859, and shows a crowned lion with staff on a pedestal with the legend, "Vryheyt," encircled by legend, "Pro patria eiusque lebertate," with crown at top.

Inscriptions: "Major John André, died Tappan, N.J. 2 Oct. 1780, aged 29. He was not commissioned major until 1780," leaf 73, in late hand; note regarding the provenance of the MS, leaf 80*v*; note regarding the life of Dr. John Greenwood, written by his son in 1845, leaf 81*v*.

The *Dictionary of American Biography* contains a brief sketch of Dr. John Greenwood, who was a fife major in Paterson's 15th Massachusetts Regiment and George Washington's personal dentist. His acquisition of the MS from a British fife major is asserted in the note by his son, leaf 81*v*; his grandson, Isaac J. Greenwood, states that the MS was taken from the Hessians at Trenton, in *The Greenwood Family of Norwich, England, in America* (Printed privately, 1934), p. 101. The son's statement, however, is considered the more accurate.

No. 975 in the *Guide to the Manuscript Collections of the New York Historical Society*, by Arthur J. Breton (Westport, Conn., Greenwood Press, 1972).

A Dictionary of Such Greek, Latin and French Words as Generally Occur in Music, verso of last numbered leaf. Index, first unnumbered leaf, continued on leaf 87*v* and completed in different hand in pencil, leaf 87*r*.

Melody only, unless otherwise indicated.

Leaf [*Versos* blank, unless otherwise indicated]

Leaf	
1	Granoms Minuet
2	Fisher's Minuet
3	Chalk's Hornpipe
	King George the Third's Minuet
4	Come Haste to the Wedding
5	Mr. Beckfords Minuet
6	Master Linley's Hornpipe
7	Mrs. Vernon's Hornpipe
8	Mr. Geises Minuet
	Duet.
9	Countess of Coventry's Minuet
	Duet.
10	God Save the King
	Duet.
11	The Prince of Wale's Minuet
	L'Oiseau royal. Cotillion
12	Come Away, Come Away
13	Over the Water to Charlie, with Variations
14	[Blank]
15	Sweet Passion of Love
16	Jack's Delight
17	Cupid God of Soft Persuasion
	Title crossed through; see leaf 18*v* below.
	The Marquis of Granby's, or 1st Troop of Hons. Grenodiers March
18*r*	[Blank]
18*v*	Cupid God of Soft Persuasion
20	On Pleasures Smooth Wings
21	Take Me Jenny
22	Lovely Nymph
23	Jockey
24*r*	[Blank]
24*v*	The Mulberry Tree

Leaf [*Versos* blank, unless other-
      wise indicated]

26   Ty Tol[?] or The Country
     Dance

27   Ye Warwickshire Lads

28   The Dorsetshire March
     Duet.

29   Grenadiers March

30   Gramachree Molly
     See also leaf 75 below.

31   Don Fisco

32   Love for Ever

33   Foots Minuet

34   Martins Minuet

35   Rosalin Castle

36   Miss Bowls's Minuet

37   Boston March
     God Save the King

38   My Dog and My Gun
     For 2d part, see leaf
     75 below.
     Jigg

39   How Imperfect is Expression
     [Untitled]
     Incomplete.

40   How Sweet thro the Woodlands

41   Love for Love

42   The London Assembly

43   Guardin Angles
     In G major; see also
     leaf 66 below.

44   Hunting Song
     Love and Oportunite

45   Maggie Lauder

46   The Drum

47   York Fuseliers

48   Successful Campain

49   The Highland Laddie

Leaf [*Versos* blank, unless other-
      wise indicated]

50   Fishers Hornpipe
     Thear is No Luck about the
     House

51   In Infancy

52   Allemand Swiss

53   Melonie's Gig

54   Cotillion
     Same melody as leaf
     59 below.

55   Constant Charly
     Minuetto

56   Farewell ye Greenfields
     Welcome Here Again

57   Flowers of Edinburgh

58   Reel
     Lovely Nancy

59   Cotillion
     Same melody as leaf
     54 above.

60   Dielson's March
     2d part added in later
     hand.

61   Allemande

62   Cotillion the Gesuit

63   The Marquis of Granby
     Boston Delight

64   Minuetto

65   Through the Wood Laddie

66   A Favourite Irish Air
     Guardin Angels
     In A major; see also
     leaf 43 above.

67   Haymaker
     O Kelly

68   Trompet Minuet
     Two versions, the latter
     incomplete.

70   Black Dancree
     Shepherds I Have Lost My Love

45. *NEW YORK: NEW YORK CITY. NEW YORK HISTORICAL SOCIETY (JOHN GREENWOOD)*

Leaf [*Versos* blank, unless other-wise indicated]

71 Highland's March
The Hessian Camp

72 Chain Cotillion

73 A Song of Major Andrea

74 Jockey to the Fair
The Free Masons March

Leaf [*Versos* blank, unless other-wise indicated]

75 Gramachree Molly
See also leaf 30 above.
Second to My Dog My Gun
For 1st part, see leaf 38 above.

78 Alloa House

79*r* Waltz
In later hand.

79*v* Di Papitati
Later hand, in pencil.

46. *NEW YORK: NEW YORK CITY. NEW YORK PUBLIC LIBRARY, RESEARCH LIBRARY FOR THE PERFORMING ARTS, MUSIC DIVISION, AMERICANA COLLECTION. *MNZ AMER. GENERAL.*

"JOHN FIELD JUNR. 1789. DUETS." 1 p., 1 leaf, [72] pp. 31 cm.

Title from cover.

Entries in various hands and inks: "A," pp. [1]-[2], [4]-[39], [44]-[56]; "B," p. [3]; "C,"pp. [40]-[43]; "D," pp. [57]-[71]; "E," p. [72] (upside down).

Inscriptions: "John Field 1790," preliminary page; "B. March 22, 1791," following gamut, p. [62]; pencilled annotations in much later hand noting printed versions of various titles, the information apparently taken from Sonneck-Upton.

Table of flats and sharps, p. [1]. Keyboard gamut, p. [62].

For 2 flutes or violins, pp. [1]-[51], unless otherwise indicated, with primo and secondo on opposite pages; the remainder includes songs and works for keyboard alone.

Page [Pagination supplied]

2 Hark Away Is the Word
The Graces
In hand "B;" melody only, p. [3].

Page [Pagination supplied]

4 Rondo
Rondo
Return from the Chase

6 March
Presto

46. *NEW YORK: NEW YORK CITY. NEW YORK PUBLIC LIBRARY (JOHN FIELD)*

Page [Pagination supplied] Page [Pagination supplied]

63 Fair Well ye Green Fields

64 The Rose Tree

65 Knip Houssen's March

66 Come Hast[e] to the Wedding

67 Drink to Me Only
    Who Killed Cock Robin?
      Who killed Cock Robin?
        Melody only.

68 La Bell Catherin
    Che' b[?]anze vous
      Dans votre lit, my Fanny
    say
        Only 1st line of
        words copied.

70 Jolly Dick the Lamplighter
    I'm jolly Dick the lamp-
    lighter, they say
        Treble and bass, includ-
        ing introduction and rit-
        ornello; vv. 2-4 as text.

72 [Untitled]
    How swift the time beguiling
    Melody only.

47. *NEW YORK: NEW YORK CITY. NEW YORK PUBLIC LIBRARY, RESEARCH
LIBRARY FOR THE PERFORMING ARTS, MUSIC DIVISION, AMERICANA
COLLECTION. JOC 72-11.*

"MICAH HAWKINS'S BOOK OF NOTES FOR THE GERMAN
FLUTE. 1794" [ii], 83 [i.e., 88] pp. 18 x 31 cm.

Cover title; additional title, p. [1]: "A
Choice Collection of Tunes for the German Flute."

One thick fold sewn into plain boards.

In Micah Hawkins' hand throughout.

Inscriptions: "November 14th 1794," p. 20;
"Here ends one hundred and four tunes, February
20th, 1795," pp. 43-44; "Wm S. Mount, August,
1841," p. [88]; "Mica[h] Hawkins," with pen and
ink sketch of the compiler at a table with book
and candle, back cover.

Cited by Wolfe, p. 350. Micah Hawkins (1777-
1825) was the uncle of the painter, William
Sidney Mount (1807-1868), who apparently was a
subsequent owner of the MS (see inscription
above); for more on their musical relationship,
see Alfred Frankenstein, *William Sidney Mount*,
pp. 80, 91, 93. This MS, as well as others later
compiled by Hawkins, are described by Vera Brodsky
Lawrence in "Micah Hawkins, the Pied Piper of
Catherine Slip," *New York Historical Society Quarterly*
62 (1978):138-65.

A Scale of All the Natural Notes, p. [ii].
Index, pp. [85]-[87].

Melody only, with the exception of the duets
"for 2 Ger[man] Flutes (pp. 23, 24, 31 below),"
which include the second part.

INSIDE All the Day
FRONT   Birds in the Aire
COVER   The White Cockade
        Ginney's Got Hair on It
        A Troop

Page

[i] Huky Muckey
     The Boin Water
     Green Groes the Rushes, Oh

[ii] London Dary
     Nancy Dorsson

 1   God Save the King
     Come Haste to the Wedding
     Comick Tune in *Orpheus and
         Euridice*
     Tune in *Apollo and Daphne*

 2   The Colledge Hornpipe
     Columbia

 3   Count Saxes March
     Hang Me if I Marry
     The Rose

 4   The Peasants Dance
     The Brick Maker
     La Promanade

 5   Marionets
     Wilke's Wriggle
     The Cuckoo's Nest

 6   The Marquis of Granby's
         March
     Come Rouse Brother

 7   Over the Water to Charlie,
         with the Variations

 8   Lovely Nymph
     Ye Warwickshire ye Lads and
         ye Lasses
     Ye Fair Possess'd

 9   Chiling o Guiry, with the
         Variations

Page

10   Mrs. Vernon's Hornpipe

11   Rose Tree
     Foots Minuets
     Brittons Strike Home
     Charming Phillis

12   Thro' the Wood Laddie
     See the Conquering Hero

13   Gavot in *Thomas and Sally*
     Away to the Field

14   Hob or Nob a Country Dance
     A Countery Dance, The White
         Joke

15   Devil's Dream
     Washington's Resign

16   Irish Billy
     New Daniel Cooper
     Shingley's Allemand

17   Clarkes Hornpipe
     Minuet in *Samson*
     The Soldiers Joy. City Dance
     The Maid of the Oak
     Paddy-Whack

18   How Oft Louisa
     Sugar a Candy

19   La Nouville Province
     Port Patrick
     La Nanoine

20   The General Toast
     The Four Seasons
     The Gentle Ohio

21   The Galley Slaves Complaint,
         or The Pilgrims Triumph
     The Pantheon Cotillion

22   Lango Lee
     The Dusky Night
     Jockey to the Fair

47. *NEW YORK: NEW YORK CITY. NEW YORK PUBLIC LIBRARY (MICAH HAWKINS)*

Page

Page

83 The Seven Stares	INSIDE Loang Toun Retreat
Enfield Wash	BACK Tug Hill
Larry Grogan	COVER Girls Take Care of Your
Satts Hole	Towrow-ron
84 [Blank]	Rose in a Castle

48. *NEW YORK: NEW YORK CITY. NEW YORK PUBLIC LIBRARY, RESEARCH LIBRARY FOR THE PERFORMING ARTS, MUSIC DIVISION, AMERICANA COLLECTION. JOB 72-1, LEDYARD, JONATHAN D.*

COMMONPLACE BOOK CONTAINING SECULAR TUNES.
[52] pp.   8 x 18.5 cm.

Half-leather library binding.

Entries apparently in same hand and ink. Watermark: shield (7.5 x 6 cm.) containing archer holding bow in one hand, arrow in the other; leaves [7] and [24] bear date, 1804.

Inscriptions: "Jonathan D. Ledyard [signature]," pp. [1], [8], [10], [23], [27]-[28], [31], [34], [37], [39(initials only)], [42], [45]-[46],[52]; "American Museum," p. [10]; "Presented by Wm Wright [or Waight?], Catskill, March 10th 1810," p. [20].

Listed as "Manuscript song tunes," in William Salloch's Catalog no. 235.

Earlier titles numbered by compiler, 1-29; some later, unnumbered titles interspersed. Index, p. [52], continued inside back cover; includes the following titles, lacking in the MS: "Canadian Volunteers," "Sweet Little Sue," "Finale to *Robin Hood*."

Melody only.

Page [Pagination supplied]

Page [Pagination supplied]

1 1. The Lee Rigg	4 7. Bellisle March
2. Bugle Horn	8. Tidii or Paddy's Wedding
2 3. Niel Gow	5 9. Quickstep
4. Swiss Guards March	10. White Cockade
3 5. The Cheat	6 [Blank]
6. Lady Shaftsbury's Strathspey	7 11. Boston March
	12. Canada Farewell

Page [Pagination supplied]		Page [Pagination supplied]	
8	13. Lord McDonald's Reel	28	[Blank]
9	13. Adams & Liberty	29	29. Bugle Horn Quick Step
	Error in numbering.	30	A March in the Waltz
	14. Yankee Doodle		Cotillion
10	[Blank]	31	[Blank]
11	15. Within a Mile of Edin-	32	Hob or Nob
	burgh	33	Lady Buckley's Whim
	16. March in *Blue Beard*	34	A Cotillion
12	17. Roslin Castle		Lacking in Index.
13	18. Gore's March	35	Slow March
	19. God Save America	36	Duke of York's Cotillion
14.	The Flower of Edinburgh	37	[Blank]
15	20. March to Boston	38	Tartan Pladdy
16	The Stranger in America	38	Duke of Portland's Waltz
17	21. Gavot by Wiedman	40	[Blank]
	22. Malbrook	41	The New Century Hornpipe
18	[Blank]	42	[Blank]
19	23. Irish Washer Woman	43	Dutchess Slipper
20	[Blank]	44	[Blank]
21	24. Pantheon Cotillion	45	Felton's Gavot
22	[Blank]		Copied in opposite
23	25. Duke of Holstein's March		direction.
24	[Blank]	46	Austrian Retreat
25	26. The Rose Tree		Copied in opposite
26	27. Quick March		direction.
	Don Quick Step	48	[Blank]
27	28. The Yellow Haired Laddie	49	The Little Sailor Boy
			Free Mason
		50	Prince Coburg's March

49. NEW YORK: NEW YORK CITY. NEW YORK PUBLIC LIBRARY, RESEARCH
     LIBRARY FOR THE PERFORMING ARTS, MUSIC DIVISION, AMERICANA
     COLLECTION. *MNZ AMER. GENERAL.

     COPYBOOK CONTAINING DUETS FOR TWO VIOLINS. 92
     [i.e., 93] pp. 34 cm.

     20th-century leather binding with original

leather label, stamped "Joseph Lewis," mounted on cover.

Entries appear to be in same hand and ink and on similar paper.

Index, p. [93], includes letters A-D only.

Violin primo and secondo copied on facing pages, except those on pp. 1 and 92, where double staves are used.

Page

1   God Save Columbia
    Farewell to Green Fields
    Away with Melancholy
    O Dear What Can the Matter Be

2   Duet. 1, by Pleyel
    Duet. 2, by Pleyel

4   Duet. 3, by Pleyel
    March in *God of Love*

6   Duet. 4, by Pleyel
    La Chontille Cotillion

8   Duet. 5, by Pleyel
    Duet. 6, by Pleyel

10 Duet. 7, by Pleyel
    Swiss Guards' March

12 Duet. 8, by Pleyel
    German Hymn, by Pleyel

14 Duet. 9, by Pleyel
    March, Allegro

16 Duet. 10, by Pleyel
    Echo

18 Duet. 11, by Pleyel
    Julia to the Wood Robin

20 Duet. 12, by Pleyel
    Cottage Maid

22 Duet. 13, by Pleyel
    Favorite Air

24 Duet. 14, by Pleyel

26 Duet. 15, by Pleyel

28 Duet. 16, by Pleyel

30 Duet. 17, by Pleyel

Page

32 Duet. 18, by Pleyel

34 Duet. 19, by Pleyel

36 Duet. 19. Continued
    Duet. 20, by Pleyel

38 Duet. 20. Continued
    Stamitz's Air

40 Duet. 21, by Pleyel

42 Duet. 21. Continued
    Duet. 22. By Pleyel

44 Duet. 22. Concluded

46 Duet. 23. By Pleyel

48 Duet. 23. Concluded
    Rondo. By Fisher
    Yellow Hair'd Lad
    French Air. No. 1

50 Duet. 24, by Pleyel

52 Duet. 24. Continued

54 French Air. No. 2
    Moreau's March
    Wayne's March
    Rake's of London

56 Duet. 25. By Pleyel
    Duet. 26. By Decamy
    Lachrimoso. Pia
    Allamande
    March

58 Rondo. By Kammell
    Air
        Index: Air Affetuoso.
    Handel's Clarionett

Page

60	Duet. 27
	The Irish Dass
	Duetto. 28
	Quick March in *Oscar*
	A Favorite Allegro
62	Allemande. No. 2. By Cyrowetz
	March in *Abaellino*
	A Favorite Allemande
	Sicilian Mariner's Hymn
64	Menuetto. By Pleyel
	Governor Strong's March
	Boston Cadet's March
66	Duet. 29, by Pleyel
	Genl. C. C. Pinckney's March
68	Capt. Sargent's Quickmarch
	Rise Cynthia, Rise
	Duet 30th. By Pleyel
70	When Tell Tale Echoes, in *Paul and Virginia*
	Favorite Polonese
	Duet 31st. By Wragg
72	Duet 32. By Wragg
	March a la Militaire
	March in *Blue Beard*
	Massachusetts March

Page

74	Duet. 33. By Stamitz
76	Duet 33. Continued
78	Slow March, No. 1. By Mumler
	Slow March, No. 2. By Mumler
80	Quick March, No. 1. By Mumler
	Quick March, No. 2. By Mumler
	Quick March, No. 3. By Mumler
	Air. Andante
82	Quick March, No. 4. By Mumler
	Menuetto. By Mumler
	German Waltz in the Time of a Minuet
	Dance in *The Honeymoon*
84	Grand March in *Lodoiska*
	Grand March, Battle of Prague
	Washington's March
	German Air. By Schultz
86	Duet. 34. By Rosencrantz
88	Duet. 34. Concluded
	Duet. 35. By Rosencrantz
90	Duet. 35. Concluded
92	Time Has Not Thin'd My Flowing Hair

50. *NEW YORK: NEW YORK CITY. NEW YORK PUBLIC LIBRARY, RESEARCH LIBRARY FOR THE PERFORMING ARTS, MUSIC DIVISION, AMERICANA COLLECTION. *MNZ AMER. GENERAL.*

COPYBOOK CONTAINING SONGS AND PIANO COMPOSITIONS. [70] pp. 30 cm.

Entries in same hand and ink and on same paper.

Manuscript words of poem, "The Grasshopper ([4] leaves)," inserted.

Songs with keyboard accompaniment, or for keyboard solo.

50. *NEW YORK: NEW YORK CITY. NEW YORK PUBLIC LIBRARY (ANON. 1)*

Page [Pagination supplied]

1 Within a Mile of Edinburgh,
   Introduced & Sung by Miss
   Broadhurst in the Musical
   Farce Called *My Grand-
   mother*
   Twas within a mile of
   Edinburgh town

2 Whither my Love
   Whither my love

4 Sonata 1; Nicolay

16 O Let the Danger of a Son -
   Dr. Arne
   O let the danger of a son

18 Song by Hook
   The day is departed

20 Fair Aurora
   Fair Aurora prithee stay

22 [Untitled] Sung by Mr.
   Tenduci
   Water parted from the sea

24 A Favorite Song, Sung by Mrs.
   Crouch in the Musical
   Romance of *Ladoiska*, by
   Storace
   Ye streams that round my
   prison creep
   V. 2 as text.

26 Whilst with Village Maids I
   Stray, [from] *Rosina*
   Whilst with village maids
   I stray

28 Song
   For keyboard.

29 The Affectionate Soldier, a
   New Ballad
   Twas in the evening of a
   wintry day
   Vv. 2-6 as text.

30 [Untitled]
   Light as thistle down

32 Song (sung by Rosetta and
   Lucinda)
   Hope! Thou nurse of
   young desire

Page [Pagination supplied]

34 Song
      Incomplete.

35 Song
   Tell me babbling echo

36 Song
   Cease your music gentle
   swains

38 [Untitled]
   Na Mair ye bonny lasses
   gay

40 Emma, or The Blooming Rose
   Lead, sweetest Emma

42 Tell Me Cruel Cupid, Rondo
   Favori
   Tell me cruel Cupid

44 Poor Tom, by Mr. Dibdin
   Here a sheer hulk lies poor
   Tom Bowling

45 The Maid of Martindale, by Hook
   In Martindale village a
   damsel deigns to dwell

46 The Wedding Day
   What virgin or shepherd in
   valley or grove
      Vv. 2-3 as text.

48 Song, by Mrs. Hodgkinson
   Primroses deck the banks
   green side

50 The Dream
   Stay, oh stay thou lovely
   shade

51 [Untitled]
   Come pretty bee

52 By This Fountains Flowry Side.
   Belville
   By this fountains flowry side

53 *Rosina*
   Taste of pleasures, ye who
   may

54 Ode to Delia
   Go to her hands

(102)

Page [Pagination supplied]

59   The Spring [from] *Poor Soldier*
     The spring with smiling face
     V. 2 as text.

60   [Untitled]
     Margaretta: With lowly suit and plaintive ditty
     V. 2 as text.

62   [Untitled]
     Adela: Be mine tender passion

Page [Pagination supplied]

66   The Cuckoo
     Charming Cuckoo, bird of spring
       Includes interludes for [flauto] traverso.

70   She Never Thinks of Me
     The morning dew that wets the rose

51.   *NEW YORK: NEW YORK CITY. NEW YORK PUBLIC LIBRARY, RESEARCH LIBRARY FOR THE PERFORMING ARTS, MUSIC DIVISION, AMERICANA COLLECTION. DREXEL 4492.*

    COPYBOOK CONTAINING HYMNS, SONGS, ETC. 60, [8] leaves. 10 x 19 cm.

      Entries apparently in same hand and ink and on same paper.

      This copybook book is listed in Sonneck-Upton, p. 247, and therefore included here; the repertory, however, is well after 1800, as Sonneck himself recognized. None of the titles is otherwise listed in Sonneck; seven are in Wolfe, with first publication dates ranging from 1801 ("Jefferson and Liberty") to 1820 ("The Whippoorwill").

      Hymns, leaves 1-40; only the secular tunes are listed below.

      Melody only.

Leaf [*Versos* blank, unless otherwise indicated]

41   The Federals March
     Burbanks March

42   The Grand Spy
     Jefferson and Liberty

43   Primrose Hill
     No Luck about [the] House

44   March to Boston
     The Blew Bird

Leaf [*Versos* blank, unless otherwise indicated]

45   The Bells of Scotland
     In the Cottage

47   Blew Eyde Mary

48   Lady Washington's Favorite
     The Grand Troop

49   Day of Glory

50r   The Federals March
     The Whippoorwill

51. *NEW YORK: NEW YORK CITY. NEW YORK PUBLIC LIBRARY (ANON. 2)*

Leaf [*Versos* blank, unless other-   Leaf [*Versos* blank, unless other-
       wise indicated]   wise indicated]

  50*v* March for Bonaparts Inperial   52*r* [Blank]
          Guard   52*v* [Untitled]

  51*r* Installation March   53-60 [Blank]

  51*v* [Untitled]

52. *NEW YORK: NEW YORK CITY. NEW YORK PUBLIC LIBRARY, RESEARCH
LIBRARY FOR THE PERFORMING ARTS, MUSIC DIVISION, AMERICANA
COLLECTION. *MN M288 AMER.*

MANUSCRIPT COLLECTION OF MARCHES, DANCES, ETC.
78 [i.e., 75] pp. 7 x 20 cm.

Title from typed label pasted in.

Library binding; pages partially and irregularly
numbered, some out of order or missing, cf.
Index. Apparently lacking Index pp. 38, 39,
59-66, 71-72.

Entries apparently in same hand and ink and on
same paper.

Index, p. [75], cites original pagination.

Melody only, except for the first entry.

Page [Pagination supplied]:Index page Page [Pagination supplied]:Index page

  1:1   ___[illegible] of Columbia   17:3 40th Regiment
        Columbia, Columbia, to Glory   Title trimmed off, but
        and ___[illegible]   supplied from Index.
          Page partially torn away;   British Muse
          alternate titles in Index:
          "Alknosnok" and "Columbia." 18:4 Duke of Holstein's March

  2:2   [Blank]   19:5 Primrose Hill
                            2d word illegible, but
  3:59   Copenhagen Waltz   supplied from Index.
 4-12:? [Blank]   Air of Critic

 13:51 King of Prussia's March   20:6 Belisle March
        Bonaparte's March   Molly Put the Kettle On

 14:52 Genl Green's March   21:7 Somebody
                            The Harriot
 15:53 Roslin Castle
                            22:8 [Blank]
 16:54 Hob or Nob
        Hay Makers   23:9 The Frog and the Mouse
          Incomplete; concluded   Hollow Drum
          on p. [63]:55 below.   Greenfields

Page [Pagination supplied]:Index page Page [Pagination supplied]:Index Page

24:10 Go to the Devil and Shake
         Yourself

25:11 Fisher's Hornpipe
         Air by Handel
         Sea Flower

26:12 [Blank]

27:13 March on the Banks of the
         Rine

28:14 [Blank]

29:15 Marche des Marseillois
         Index: "Marselles
         March."

30:16 [Blank]

31:17 Mason's Farewell
         Yankee Doodle

32:18 [Blank]

33:19 The Independent Rangers
         Heathen Mythology, or
         Hunting the Hare

34:20 [Blank]

35:21 March to Boston
         Serenade

36:22 [Blank]

37:23 White Cockade
         Mary's Dream

38:24 [Blank]

39:25 Galley Slave
         Myrtle Grove, or Widners
         Whim

40:26 [Blank]

41:27 Mersailles Hymn
         My Life is a___[illegible]
         of Freedom Plase

42:28 [Blank]

43:29 Rose Tree

44:30 [Blank]

45:31 Banks of Flowers
         Rural Felicity

46:32 [Blank]

47:33 American March

48:34 [Blank]

49:35 General Greens March
         Blaize at Babet

50:36 [Blank]

51:37 New Colisheam's March
         Felton's Air, or Herald of
             Muses
             Index gives alternate title
             as principal.
         Unhappy Swain

52:40 [Blank]

53:41 Governor Jays March
         Index: "Jay's March."

54:42 [Blank]

55:43 Boss [or Bob?] Middletown
         Note[?] bien[?] Forsaken Man
             Index: "Forsaken Maid"
             crossed through, but written
             in again.
         Apollo Turned Sheperd

56:44 [Blank]

57:45 The Young Widow
         Shays March

58:46 Hail Columbia

59:47 Vous la donnez
         Dusky Night

60:48 [Blank]

61:49 Yeo! Yeo! Yeo! [?]
             Illegible here and in
             Index.
         Waldecker's March

62:50 [Blank]

63:55 [Continuation of Hay Makers,
             p. [16]:54 above].

63:55 Duke of York's March

64:56 Jefferson & Liberty

65:57 Bluebeard
             Index: "March in Bluebeard."
         Soldier's Return

52. *NEW YORK: NEW YORK CITY. NEW YORK PUBLIC LIBRARY (ANON. 3)*

Page [Pagination supplied]:Index page Page [Pagination supplied]:Index page

66:58 Lesson by Morelli

67-72:77-78, 67-70
    [Blank]

73:73 [Untitled]
      In pencil.

74:74 [Blank]

53. *NEW YORK: ROCHESTER. UNIVERSITY OF ROCHESTER, EASTMAN SCHOOL OF MUSIC, SIBLEY MUSIC LIBRARY. M 1.A1 C697.*

"NANCY BROWN. SEP. 1ST, 1796." [58] pp.
21 x 25 cm.

Title from label pasted on cover.

Entries probably in same hand and ink, except in "Rise, Cynthia Rise," and on same kind of paper.

Copybook containing repertory chiefly of works first published in Philadelphia between 1790 and 1800.

Songs and keyboard music (solo and duets); the songs scored on 2 staves for treble (1 or 2 parts) and bass, often with keyboard introduction and postlude.

Page

1 Lovely Spring
   The lovely spring advancing

4 The Lass of Richmond Hill
   On Richmond hill there
   lives a lass

6 The Gem of Aberdeen

7 My Friend and Pitcher

8 [Untitled keyboard duets,
   one attributed by the
   compiler to Shuster]

16 When William at Eve
   When William at eve meets
   me down at the stile

18 Ode on the Death of Dr.
   Franklin
   The fairest flowrets bring
   in all their vernal bloom

19 Major André's Complaint
   Return enraptur'd hours

Page

20 *The Purse, or Benevolent Tar*
   When a little merry he
   Includes introduction with
   indication of orchestral
   flutes, and "Symphony"
   following the first two
   lines.

22 The Twins of Latona
   The twins of Latona

25 Sweet Lilies of the Valley
   O'er barren hills and
   flow'ry dales
   V. 2 as text.

27 Evening
   Ere night assumes her gloomy
   reign
   V. 2 as text.

29 Overture of *The Desserteure*

30 Hymn III. Chatham
   Jesus lover of my soul

Page

Page

31 Willy Far Away. A Celebrated
        New Song Composed by
        Mr. Hook
        My love the pride of hill
        and plain

33 Rise, Cynthia Rise. By
        Mr. Hook
        Rise, Cynthia rise
        Duet; includes a middle
        section copied by a less
        tutored hand entitled
        "Air."

36 The Silver Moon. By Mr. Hook
        Where shall I see the
        lovely swain

38 May Day Morn. A Favorite
        Sonnet Composed by
        Mr. Hook
        Sweet music wakes the May
        day morn

40 The Black Bird. By Mr. Hook
        'Twas on a bank of daisies
        sweet
            Vv. 2-5 as text.

42 Hark the Herald Angels Sing
        Hark the herald angels sing

44 The Galley Slave
        O think on my fate

46 The Hollow Drum
        When the hollow drum has
        beat to bed

50 The Way Worn Traveller
        Faint and weary the way worn
        traveller pleads
            Duet between "Agnes" and
            "Ladi."

54 O Innocence Celestial Maid. Sung
        by Mrs. Warrel
        O innocence celestial maid

56 Lowland Laddie
        Of all the swains both far
        and near

54. *PENNSYLVANIA: PHILADELPHIA.   FREE LIBRARY, MUSIC DIVISION.*
     [*UNCATALOGED MS*]

     "ARMONIA DOMESTICA." Vocal score (21pp.); parts
     for flute (5 pp.) and violoncello (4 pp.) 30 cm.
     (score); 29 cm. (parts).

         Title from binder's label stamped in gold on
         front cover of parts only.

         Score and parts bound in half-leather over
         boards; parts have marbled paper and binder's
         label.

         Probably in the hand of Benjamin Carr, entered
         into the first few pages of copybooks in which
         all remaining leaves are blank but ruled.

         Inscriptions: "B. Carr [signature]," p. 1 (score
         and parts); "192" (score), "237" (flute part),
         and "190" (violoncello part), inside front
         covers. For MSS similarly numbered in Carr's hand,

54. *PENNSYLVANIA: PHILADELPHIA. FREE LIBRARY (ARMONIA DOMESTICA)*

see Nos. 34, 35, 62, 64, and 65.

Nos. 3-6 below were issued by Carr between 1794 and 1799, according to Sonneck-Upton, as songs with keyboard. In these MS copies the parts are all in keys lower than those of the score, except for No. 3.

For voice and piano or harp as indicated below, with apparently optional flute and violoncello.

Page [Pagination of vocal score only]		Page [Pagination of vocal score only]	
2	No. 1. Words & Music Mr. Ellis Oh! Why should I weep For voice and harp; flute and violoncello parts indicated in cadential sections; 2 vv.	9	No. 4. Welch Air Tho' far beyond the mountains For voice and harp; 3 vv.
4	No. 2. Carr Adieu ye streams that sweetly flow For voice and harp; 2 vv.	16	No. 5. Carr - Words by Harwood When nights were cold For voice and harp; flute introduction indicated; vv. 2-3 as text.
6	No. 3. Webbe Soft zephyr on thy balmy wing For voice and piano; flute and violoncello parts indicated in introduction; 2 vv.	19	No. 6. Carr - Words by Harwood See from your cottage For voice and piano; vv. 2-3 as text.

55. *PENNSYLVANIA: PHILADELPHIA. FREE LIBRARY, MUSIC DIVISION. MANU-SCRIPTS FROM THE ESTATE OF BENJAMIN CARR.*

COPYBOOK CONTAINING MANUSCRIPT AND PRINTED MUSIC. 200 [i.e., 214] pp. 35 cm.

Bound in half-leather and marbled paper over boards.

Various hands, inks, and papers (trimmed to uniform size for binding). A clearly later hand begins p. 177. The paper of pp. [208] and [209] is a much later 19th-century paper, but contains a continuation, in the same hand, of the variations beginning p. [207]. Various watermarks: pp. 130-37 dated 1794; pp. 1 and last flyleaf have same watermark, the former dated 1798; sheet laid between pp. 21 and 22 bears initials "E & P" and date, 1795; sheet pinned between pp. 117 and

118 bears name, "W. Young," and date, 1804.

Inscriptions: "Written by F. Hopkinson, Esq., 1798," p. 21; "See Col. Hist. v. 10, p. 201," p. 110; "August the 14 1800," p. 114.

This MS contains repertory ranging in date from first British publication of 1780 (pp. 2-14) to the dedication, "For the 4th July 1826 (entitled, "Himno patiotica guerro, compuesto por el cuidadano patriota, J. M. C.," beginning, "Illustres Americanos,"p. [211])." The bulk of the music, however, falls in the decade between 1795 and 1805. Although such works as the songs by Thomas Moore (pp. 135-37) are presumably well after 1800, they are written on paper bearing a 1794 watermark and are surrounded by works that could have been copied earlier than 1800. The inventory, therefore, will stop at p. 180, because there is a clear break in both hand (p. 177) and repertory (pp. 196ff.): the first two works in the later hand (pp. 177-80) reflect the earlier repertory and pp. 181-95 contain songs and arias in French and Italian attributed to various European composers. Beyond this point the repertory is clearly after 1805.

Index: p. 1. Printed items from Carr's *Musical Journal*, pp. 2-11. Instructions for "just" tuning of the harpsichord, verso of last fly-leaf.

Chiefly for voice and piano.

Page

12 The Celebrated Chaccone or
Spanish Dance,Composed
by Sigr Jomelli
For keyboard.

14 Hymn of Praise
Lo He comes with clouds
descending
2 parts (soprano and
alto) with figured bass.
Hymn: Meditation
Jesus! and shall it ever
be a mortal man
Figured bass.

15 Recitative & Air in the
Comic Opera of *La
Cosarar*

Page

(Composed by Sigr Corri)
[Recit.] Chi mai cirai, che
in questi rozzi
[Aria] Ah perche formar
non lice

18 Rondo Air Ecossais
For keyboard.

19 [Untitled]
Cruelle non, jamais.

21 The Favorite New Federal Song,
Adapted to the President's
March
Hail Columbia happy land
Vv. 2-5 as text on seper-
ate sheet tipped in.

Page

22 Duke of York's March
For keyboard.

23 The Favorite Additional
Rondo in *The Castle of
Andalusia*, Sung by
Sigr[a] Sestini; composed
by Sigr. Giordani
If I my heart surrender
English words with
Italian written above
the stave ("Mi sento
nel mio seno").

25 [Title trimmed off]
Per pietà padron mio

27 [Title trimmed off]
Quel beau jour

29 Song in the Opera of *The
Flitch of Bacon*
No, twas neither shape nor
feature
V. 2 as text.

30 Song in *Blue Beard*, Composed
by Mr. Kelly
Fatima: When pensive I
thought of my love
V. 2 as text.

31 Crazy Jane, a Favorite Ballad
Why fair maid
Vv. 2-4 as text.

32 A Prey to Anguish
A prey to tender anguish
Vv. 2-3 as text.

33 A Hymn
Before Jehovah's awful
throne

35 [Untitled]
M'ha detto la mia mama

36 [Printed songs]

73 [Blank]

74 Song in *The Pirates*
Peaceful slumb'ring on
the ocean
V. 2 as text.

Page

75 [Printed songs]

79 Une valse, by A C Vion
I.e., Charles Antoine
Vion? (BUC). See also
p. 101 below.

80 [Printed songs]

93 [Untitled gigue]

94 [Blank]

95 [Printed songs]

97 Hark the Goddess Diana
Hark the Goddess Diana
For 2 treble voices and
bass; v. 2 as text.

99 [Printed songs]

101 Un valse, par Vion
See also p. 79 above.

[101a] [Title page of printed song]
Omitted in pagination.

102 The Wood Robin
Stay sweet enchanter
For voice and keyboard
with flute or violin *ad
libitum*.

104 [Printed song]

106 Ye Ling'ring Winds
Ye ling'ring winds that
feebly blow
Vv. 2 and 6 as text.

108 [Printed song]

110 Col. Burrows's March
Allemande

111 [Printed song]

114 [Blank staves]

115 [Printed song]

117 The Death Song of the Cherokee
Indians
The sun sets in [i.e., at]
night

Page

[Sheet pinned in; see note above
          regarding watermark.]
     The Dying Lamb. Music by
          a Young Lady
          A new fallen lamb

118 [Printed songs]

123 Ariette
          En amour c'est au village
          Vv. 2-3 as text.

124 [Printed song]

125 Roy's wife
          Roy's wife of Aldivaloch
          Vv. 2-3 as text.

126 Romance
          Bouton de rose
          V. 2 as text.

127 [Printed works dated March
          1801]

129 Overture to *Lodoiska*, by
          Stephen Storace
          For keyboard; figured bass.

132 German Walz
          For keyboard.

133 The Resolution, by Mozart
          Ye gentle gales that care-
          less blow
               Includes written-out
               cadenzas

135 Oh Lady Fair. Music and Words
          by T. Moore Esq.
          Oh lady fair
               Vocal duet with keyboard;
               v. 2 as text.

137 Music & Words by T. Moore
          Esq.
          When time who steals our
          years

138 Begone dull care
          Begone dull care

Page

139 [Songs and arias in French and
          Italian, attributed to
          various European composers]

172 [Blank staves]

173 Les yeux bleux
          Aimés ces yeux noirs
          V. 2 as text.

174 Portuguese Hymn
          O hither ye faithful
          Latin words, "Adeste
          fidelis," superscribed,
          with vv. 2-3 as text; v. 2
          of English as text.

175 Le reveil du peuple
          For keyboard.
     The New Coldstream or German
          March
          For keyboard.

176 Duncan Gray
          For keyboard, but extra
          sheet pinned in containing
          words beginning "Let not
          woman e'er complain" (i.e.,
          different from those cited
          for this title in Sonneck-
          Upton, p. 117, and Wolfe,
          nos. 2601-2 and 5139-40;
          3 vv.

177 Song from *Lodoiska* by Storace
          Ye streams that round my
          prison creep
          V. 2 as text.

179 Clementi's Grand Waltz
          For keyboard.

56. *PENNSYLVANIA: PHILADELPHIA. FREE LIBRARY, MUSIC DIVISION. MANU-SCRIPT MUSIC FROM THE ESTATE OF BENJAMIN CARR.*

COPYBOOK CONTAINING MUSIC CHIEFLY FOR KEYBOARD. [i], [122] pp. 30 cm.

Bound in half-leather and marbled paper over boards; 3 leaves excised between pp. [70] and [71], and 2 leaves between pp. [75] and [76]. The second Hüllmandel Sonata (see below) is incorrectly bound.

Entries in same hand and ink and on same paper, except for pp. [42]-[56].

Inscriptions: "WTP Carr is often listed in Devon histories. I doubt that he ever came to America. He must have been a contemporary of Benjamins or perhaps a pupil of Joseph's [Benjamin's father]," note laid in before p. [1]; "Composed by M. Hullmandel, Opera the 11th, belonging to Wm Thos. Penng Carr, 31st of Decem. 1788," p. [1]. "Copied correctly," p. [11].

The MS is bound with 3 printed items, all published in London without dates but cited in BUC as between ca. 1765 and 1800. Two further printed items, identified in the Index, are lacking. All five works are for keyboard.

Index, p. [1].

For keyboard, unless otherwise indicated.

Page [Pagination supplied]

1 Two Sonatas for the Piano or Harpsichord with Accompaniments for One Violin ad libitum

24 Sonata 3d [by] Scarlatti
  Not in Index.

28 Aria del Signor Adolfo Hasse
  Quoniam si volu

30 [Blank staves]

33 Sonatina
  For flute and keyboard.
  Index identifies composer as "Charles Wesley."

Page [Pagination supplied]

38 Andante pastorale
  For 2 melody instruments and bass.

39 [Blank staves]

42 Sonata 5
  Index identifies composer as "Edelman."

56 [Blank staves]

58 Sonata 3d [by] Eckard – 1st book

71 [Blank staves]

57. *PENNSYLVANIA: PHILADELPHIA. FREE LIBRARY, MUSIC DIVISION, MANU-*
SCRIPT MUSIC FROM THE ESTATE OF BENJAMIN CARR.

COPYBOOK CONTAINING MUSIC FOR KEYBOARD. [14]
leaves. 20 x 25 cm.

Bound in brown tooled leather over boards.

Entries in same hand and ink and on same paper.

Inscriptions: "Sept. 3 1739," leaf [6*v*]; "A
now Month the 8. of October," leaf [10].

Carr was born in England in 1768; this would
therefore appear to be a MS that he either
inherited or acquired by gift or purchase.

For keyboard.

Leaf [Numbering supplied; *versos* blank]		Leaf [Numbering supplied; *versos* blank]	
1	The March in *Scipio*	7	Menuet
2	The Dying Swan Twas on a river Textual incipit only.	8	The Lass of Peaty's Mill, So Bonny Blithe and Gay
3	Prince Eugens March	9	Menuet
4	Princess Royal	10	From Mr. Bachelbels: Bass Menuet
5	King George's March	11	Jigg by Mr. Schükhardt
6	Menuet Trumpet Air	12	Menuet
		13	Psalm the 8. St. Marys
		14	100. Psalms

58. *PENNSYLVANIA: PHILADELPHIA. FREE LIBRARY, MUSIC DIVISION. MANU-*
SCRIPT MUSIC FROM THE ESTATE OF BENJAMIN CARR.

COPYBOOK CONTAINING SONGS AND KEYBOARD MUSIC.
[70] pp. 22 x 30 cm.

Worn paper covers surrounding roughly side-
stitched signatures containing two collections
of apparently different origin: the first (pp.
[1]-[32]) is water-stained, and partially and
irregularly paged, indicating an earlier, different arrangement; the second (pp. [33]-[70])
lacks pagination and is entirely in a new hand.
Leaves have been excised between pp. [16] and
[17], [28] and [29], [30] and [31], [32] and
[33], and [46] and [47].

Entries in various hands specified below in the

inventory: "A" is possibly Roth's (see first inscription and p. [25] below) and "B" possibly Schwartz's (see inscriptions pp. [1] and [8] below). Various inks. Two different sizes and stocks of paper.

Inscriptions: a receipt, referring to "Mademoissaile Sussano," with dates Sept. 3-8, 10, 12-15, 17-20, 24-26, and 28,"settled in full the 29 Sept. 1798, Philip Roth [signature]," inside front cover; "Conrad Schwartz 1800 Love," p. [1]; C. Schwartz 1801," p. [8].

Philip Roth was active as a teacher and composer in Philadelphia in 1771 and again from 1785 to his death in 1804 (see Sonneck-Upton, p. 523); the March (i.e. "Hail Columbia"), p. [5], was formerly attributed to him.

Dance figures, pp. [64], [66], and [68]. Index, p. [32], covered over by "Washington's March," in a single occurance of an untutored hand.

For keyboard, unless otherwise indicated.

Page	[Supplied pagination: original pagination]	Hand	Page	[Supplied pagination: original pagination]	Hand
1:7	Moderato	B	14:2	March [in] *The God of Love*	A
	Murcky	B	15:15	Gigue	B
2:8	The Feaderation	A	16:16	[Blank]	
	See also p. [66] below.		17:17	Aria	B
3:9	Aria	B		Allegretto	B
	The Fair America	A	18	[Blank]	
4:10	[Blank]		20:18	March	B
5:5	March	B	21	Aria	
6:6	[Blank]		22	[Title illegible due to staining]	B
7:11	Menuet [and] Trio	B		La belle Cathrine	B
8:12	[Blank]	B		In C major; see also p. [45] below.	
9:13	Menuet [and] Trio	B	23	March	B
10:14	[Blank]		24	Duke of York's March [and] Trio	A
11:13	Aria [with] Prelude for F-natural[sign]	B	25	Rondo by Phi Roth / or / Allamando	A
12:14	Under hundert tausend schönen	C	26	[Blank]	
13:1	Angl:	B			
	March	B			

Page	[Pagination supplied]	Hand
27	Bestile [i.e., Be Still]	A
	Soft Murmurs	
	Bestile soft murmurs of	
	each burling rile	
	V. 2 as text.	
28	[Title illegible due to	B
	staining]	
29	March of Marseille	B
30	____[illegible] Van Halls	A
	[i.e. Vanhal's] Rondo	
31	Grl. Hipp[?]oussen's [i.e.,	A
	Kniphausen's?] March	
	[and] Prelude for D:#	
32	Washington's March	D
33	[Continuation of preceding	E
	excised page]	
	The Black Dance	E
34	The Irish Washer Woman	E
	Come Haste to the Wedding	E
35	Catches & Glies	E
36	How Sweet thro the Wood-	E
	lands	
	How sweet thro the wood-	
	lands	
37	One Fond Kiss before We	E
	Part	
	One fond kiss before we	
	part	
38	Eliza / or / Lovely Nymph	E
	Lo[ve]ly nymph as[s]uage	
	my anguish	
39	A Favourite March	E
	March	E
40	Fisher's Hornpipe	E
41	March Ieseware[?]	E
42	The New German Spaa	E
	Jove & His Chiar [i.e.,	E
	Chair]	
44	The Huron's March	E
45	La Bell Catherina	E
	In D major; see also	
	p. [22] above.	

Page	[Pagination supplied]	Hand
46	Menuet	E
47	[Blank]	
48	Sagt wo sind die Veilgen hin	E
49	[Blank]	
50	An English Dance	E
51	The Blue Bell of Scotland	E
52	[Untitled fragment]	E
	Beginning of next tune,	
	crossed through.	
53	Ach Schwing___[illegible]	E
	Din Din___[illegble]	
54	[Blank]	
55	[Untitled fragment]	E
	Beginning of melody only.	
56	[Untitled]	E
57	[Blank]	
58	Rise Cynthia Rise	E
59	Washington's Trenton March	E
	Incomplete.	
60	[Untitled fragment]	E
	E're around the huge oak	
	V. 2 as text.	
62	[Untitled]	E
	Young Henry was as brave a	
	youth	
63	The Chase	E
64	The Pantaloon	E
65	Lesson for the Halfnotes.	E
	By Pleyel	
66	The Federation	E
	See also p. [2] above.	
67	[Untitled]	E
	Minuet and trio.	
68	L'Armadilla	E
69	The Black Forest	E
70	The Lass of Richmounth Hill	E

59. *PENNSYLVANIA: PHILADELPHIA. FREE LIBRARY, MUSIC DIVISION. MANU-SCRIPT MUSIC FROM THE ESTATE OF BENJAMIN CARR.*

EXCERPT FROM COPYBOOK CONTAINING ARIAS AND
KEYBOARD DANCES. [8] pp. 32 cm.

Single signatures from previously bound volume.

Entries in same hand and ink and on same paper.

Inscription: "Shield,"p. [1], in pencil.

Although it has been suggested that this MS may
have an association with, even be in the hand
of, Alexander Reinagle, who arranged the arias
below for publication about 1789, the evidence
is slight, especially considering the popularity
of William Shield's operas. In Reinagle's
collection, published for him not by Carr but by
J. Aitken (see Sonneck, p. 69), the three arias
below are in reverse order.

The first two arias below are from Shield's
Poor Soldier. The last(p. [6]) is attributed in
Reinagle's collection (p. 11) to "Sigr. Giordani[probably Tommaso, then a popular composer
for the London stage] in the favorite opera of
Amintas." The opera is in fact by George Rush,
and is an adaption of his *The Royal Shepherd* (1764),
staged at Covent Garden in 1769 by G. F. Tenducci,
who replaced half the arias with Italian ones
(see Roger Fiske, *English Theatre Music in the Eighteenth Century*, pp. 311-12). Thus, Reinagle's
attribution of the single aria may be correct.

For voice and keyboard or keyboard alone.

Page [Pagination supplied]	Page [Pagination supplied]
1 [Title trimmed off] The spring with smiling face	6 [Title trimmed off] Altho Heav'n['s] good pleasure
2 [Title trimmed off] The twins of Latona	7 [Untitled minuet] Danie [or Dance?]
	8 [Untitled] Minuetto

60. *PENNSYLVANIA: PHILADELPHIA. FREE LIBRARY, MUSIC DIVISION. MANU-SCRIPT MUSIC FROM THE ESTATE OF BENJAMIN CARR.*

EXCERPT FROM COPYBOOK CONTAINING MISCELLANEOUS
SONGS AND KEYBOARD MUSIC. [6] pp. 32 cm.

Loose leaves from previously bound collection.

Entries in same hand and ink and on same paper.

For keyboard (treble and bass), unless otherwise indicated.

Page [Pagination supplied]   Page [Pagination supplied]

1   [Untitled March]   4   [Title trimmed off]
    Capt. Blodget's March   Gigue?

2   [Untitled fragment]   5   Knox's March
      See p. [3] below.   College Hornpipe

3   [Untitled]   6   [Title trimmed off]
    Peaceful slumbering on   Thou art my portion O Lord
    the ocean   Incomplete.
      Alternate ending and v.2
      as text, p. [2] above.

61. *PENNSYLVANIA: PHILADELPHIA. FREE LIBRARY, MUSIC DIVISION.*
     [UNCATALOGED MS]

     "BRING FLOWERS."   [2] pp. 29 cm.

     Single sheet, music copied on both sides.

     For voice and keyboard; vv. 2-4 as text.

     First line: Bring flowers, young flowers

62. *PENNSYLVANIA: PHILADELPHIA. FREE LIBRARY, MUSIC DIVISION.*
     [UNCATALOGED MS]

     "HUSHED ARE THE WAVES."   [3] pp. 30 cm.

     Inscription: "159," p. [1]. For MSS similarly
     numbered in the hand of Benjamin Carr, see Nos.
     34, 35, 54, 64, and 65.

     For voice and keyboard (treble and bass), with
     indication of flute *ad libitum.*

     First line: Hushed are the waves

63. *PENNSYLVANIA: PHILADELPHIA. FREE LIBRARY, MUSIC DIVISION. MANU-
     SCRIPT MUSIC FROM THE ESTATE OF BENJAMIN CARR.*

     "THE ROSE, WITH AN ACCOMPANIMENT FOR THE HARPE."
     [2] pp. 30 cm.

63. *PENNSYLVANIA: PHILADELPHIA. FREE LIBRARY ("THE ROSE")*

    Single sheet, music copied on p. [1] only.

    The words are by William Cowper and were set to music (published in London) by William Crotch (ca. 1790), "Mr. Knowles (1793)," Benjamin Milgrove (1785), and Samuel Webbe, the Elder (3 editions, 1785-95). Carr published a version of the Webbe setting as a song with piano accompaniment in his *Musical Journal for the Pianoforte* [4] ([1802-3]), no. 75, pp. 10-11; see Wolfe no. 9677.

    For voice and harp; appears to be incomplete.

    First line: The rose had been wash'd

64. *PENNSYLVANIA: PHILADELPHIA. FREE LIBRARY, MUSIC DIVISION. [UNCATALOGED MS]*

    "A SAILOR'S TALE. SHIELD." [4] pp. 29 cm.

    Not intended to be bound: copied on pp. [2-3-4-1], in that order.

    Inscription: "160," p. [2]. For MSS similarly numbered in the hand of Benjamin Carr, see Nos. 34, 35, 54, 62, and 65.

    Listed by Sonneck-Upton under title, "The Post Captain," by William Shield, "sung by Mr. Incledon at the Theatre Royal, Covent Garden" (New York: 1799-1803?).

    For voice and keyboard.

    First line: When Steerwell heard me first impart

65. *PENNSYLVANIA: PHILADELPHIA. FREE LIBRARY, MUSIC DIVISION. MANUSCRIPT MUSIC FROM THE ESTATE OF BENJAMIN CARR.*

    UNTITLED KEYBOARD MUSIC, "ANDANTE." [2] pp. 31 cm.

    Single sheet with title trimmed off; music copied on p. [1] only.

    Probably in the hand of Benjamin Carr.

    Inscription: "161," p. [1]; for MSS similarly numbered in Carr's hand, see Nos. 34, 35, 54, 62, and 64.

66. *PENNSYLVANIA: PHILADELPHIA. FREE LIBRARY, MUSIC DIVISION.*
    [*UNCATALOGED MS*]

    [UNTITLED SONG. 2] pp. 26 cm.

      Single sheet, music copied on p. [1] only.

      Melody only; vv. 2-3 as text.

      First line: Round love's elysian bowers

67. *PENNSYLVANIA: PHILADELPHIA. UNIVERSITY OF PENNSYLVANIA, CHARLES
    PATTERSON VAN PELT LIBRARY, RARE BOOK DIVISION. CURTIS COLL-
    ECTIONS, 66.*

    MUSIC COPIED AT END OF *THE CONSTITUTIONS OF THE
    FREE-MASONS*... (LONDON, ANNO 5723; REPRINTED [BY
    BENJAMIN FRANKLIN] IN PHILADELPHIA...ANNO DOMINI
    1734). [27] pp. 21 cm.

      Bound in brown leather with red stamp on
    covers: "Glasgow, Johnston Killwining Lodge.
    No. 2;" therefore probably bound in Scotland
    or England.

      Entries in same hand and ink and on same paper.

      Inscriptions: "To Brother William McKinie...
    This Book of Constitutions with the Musick annex'd
    is presented by...Archd. Govane, late Mr. of
    Greenoch Kilwining, Edinburgh 25th October 1743.
    A. M. 5743," on first fly-leaf; "Richard Pate-
    shall[?] Boston. 1734," twice on title page;
    "Edinburgh 7th December 1739," on last fly-leaf;
    "Imported from London to New York October 1855,"
    in pencil, inside back cover.

      The date of the Philadelphia imprint, together
    with the phrase, "with the Musick annex'd" in
    the first inscription, suggest terminal dates of
    1734-1743 for this MS's compilation. The second
    inscription reveals that the MS could have been
    copied in Boston, although Dr. Otto E. Albrecht
    (Librarian Emeritus, University of Pennsylvania,
    Otto E. Albrecht Music Library) believes that the
    Masonic tunes are all of English origin. Songs
    from *Demetrius*, by G. B. Pescetti (see pp. [2]-[3]
    below) were published by Walsh in London in 1737.

      For keyboard (treble and bass), or voice and
    keyboard.

67. *PENNSYLVANIA: PHILADELPHIA. UNIVERSITY OF PENNSYLVANIA (FREEMASON MUSIC)*

Page [Pagination supplied]

Page	[Pagination supplied]
1	We Have No Idle Prating
2	Air in *Demetrius*
4	[Untitled] Glorius craft which fires the mind
5	To All Who Masonry Despise, &c.
6	Senesino [or Senefino?]
8	The Mason's Anthem
10	The Masters Musick
12	On On My Dear Brethren &c.

Page [Pagination supplied]

Page	[Pagination supplied]
14	The Fellow Crafts Song
16	The Prentices's Song Masons Anthom
18	[Untitled] 2 treble parts with figured bass.
20	Air in *Ariadne*
22	Air in *Porus*: Minuet
24	Minuet
26	[Untitled minuet]

68. *PENNSYLVANIA: PHILADELPHIA. UNIVERSITY OF PENNSYLVANIA, CHARLES PATTERSON VAN PELT LIBRARY, RARE BOOK DIVISION. MS. MUSIC 8.*

"MEDLEY OVERTURE. J[AMES] HEWITT." 4 parts. 34 cm.

Loose folios and leaves.

In composer's hand; ca. 1800 (cataloger's note).

In C major. The Library holds an additional autograph Medley Overture by James Hewitt with this instrumentation in D minor (Ms. Music 13); this is dated 1802 on the title page and is the same as (but differs slightly from) the one published in two editions, ca. 1802-1803 (see Wolfe nos. 3762-63).

For 2 violins, viola, and violoncello.

69. *PENNSYLVANIA: PHILADELPHIA. UNIVERSITY OF PENNSYLVANIA, CHARLES PATTERSON VAN PELT LIBRARY, RARE BOOK DIVISION. MS. MUSIC 11.*

"MEDLEY OVERTURE. A[LEXANDER] R[EINAGLE]." 4 parts. 34 cm.

Loose folios and leaves.

Possibly in composer's hand; 179-? (cataloger's note).

For 2 violins, viola, and bass.

70. *PENNSYLVANIA: PHILADELPHIA. UNIVERSITY OF PENNSYLVANIA, CHARLES PATTERSON VAN PELT LIBRARY, RARE BOOK DIVISION. MS. MUSIC 10.*

"MISCELLANEOUS OVERTURE. [ALEXANDER] REINAGLE." 4 parts. 34 cm.

Loose folios and leaves.

Possibly in composer's hand; 179-? (cataloger's note).

For 2 violins, viola, and bass; oboe part lacking.

71. *PENNSYLVANIA: PHILADELPHIA. UNIVERSITY OF PENNSYLVANIA, CHARLES PATTERSON VAN PELT LIBRARY, RARE BOOK DIVISION. MS. MUSIC 12.*

OVERTURE FOR STRINGS. 4 parts. 34 cm.

Loose folios and leaves.

Probably by Alexander Reinagle, and cataloged under his name with a question-mark.

Possibly in composer's hand; 179-? or 180-? (cataloger's note).

For 2 violins, viola and bass.

72. *PENNSYLVANIA: PHILADELPHIA. UNIVERSITY OF PENNSYLVANIA, CHARLES PATTERSON VAN PELT LIBRARY, RARE BOOK DIVISION. MS. MUSIC 9.*

"OVERTURE TO *HARLEQUINS INVASION*. MR. [ALEXANDER] REINAGLE." 4 parts. 31 cm.

Title on first violin part: Medley Overture.

Loose folios and leaves.

Possibly in composer's hand; ca. 1796 (cataloger's note).

Sonneck-Upton, p. 179, evidently quoting from an advertisement, notes that *Harlequin's Invasion*, a speaking pantomime by David Garrick, was first performed in Philadelphia on June 12, 1795, "with the original music, the accompaniments by Mr. Gillingham, with an entire new medley overture by Mr. Reinagle;" apparently it was never published.

For 2 violins, viola, and bass.

73. *RHODE ISLAND: PROVIDENCE. BROWN UNIVERSITY, JOHN HAY LIBRARY, HARRIS COLLECTION. MUSIC BY 894, RARE BOOKS.*

COPYBOOK CONTAINING SONGS AND DANCES. [i.], 114 pp. 21 x 26 cm.

Bound in heavy cardboard cover. Includes parts of two pages from the *Philadelphia Gazeteer & Universal Daily Advertiser*: dated 19th July 1797, pasted on front end-paper; dated 24th June, 1797, on p. 114. Pp. 84-87 and 98-101 omitted in pagination; pp. 16-21 and 48-49 excised.

Entries in same hand (except possibly for pp. 7-8) and ink and on same paper.

Inscriptions: "Miss Ellen Maria Byrne, No. 86 South Front Street, Philadelphia," p. 113; "Ellen Byrne," "Ellen Ann Maria Byrne," and "Miss Eleanor Maria Byrne," [signatures], *passim*; "Half of the book is written in," pp. 59-60.

This last inscription has led William Dineen to conclude that the MS originally contained 120 pp.; see his "Early American Music Manuscript Books," p. 54, n. 11. Dineen surmises that Miss Byrne was probably the daughter of Patrick Byrne, "gentleman," listed at the Front Street address after 1791, the date of the earliest directory available to him.

Rudiments, pp. 65-66. The Ground of Music Call'd Terrough Bass [i.e., rules for thorough-bass], p. 114.

Songs and duets scored for voice(s) and keyboard (treble and bass) with instrumental interlude, unless otherwise noted; remaining works for keyboard alone (treble and bass).

Page		Page	
[i]	Caledonian Reel	9	Evening
			Ere night assumes her gloomy reign
1	Duetto		
	The blushes of the morn	11	Henry's Cottage Maid
	For 2 treble parts and bass.		Ah! where can fly my soul's true love
			Vv. 2-3 as text.
3	*The Purse, or Benevolent Tar*		
	When a little merry he	13	Hush Ev'ry Breeze
			Hush ev'ry breeze
5	Ma bella coquette		
	Ma belle coquette	22	Country Dance
7	Our Pleasure	23	[Untitled]
	The Feaderation		No flow'r that blows

73. *RHODE ISLAND: PROVIDENCE. BROWN UNIVERSITY (E. M. BYRNE)*

Page

77 When Cupid Holds the Myrtle
Crown
When Cupid holds the
myrtle crown

79 How Sweet the Love That
Meets Return
When first I ken'd young
Sandy's fair

80 Byrnes' Fancy

81 When First This Humble Roof
I Knew
When first this humble
roof I knew

82 Durang's Hornpipe

83 When Rural Lads and Lassies
Gay
When rural lads and lassies
gay

88 The Highland Reel

89 I'd Rather Be Excused
Returning from the fair
one eve

Page

91 Was I a Shepherds Maid to Keep
Was I a shepherd maid to
keep on yonder plain

97 Washington's March

102 Mrs. Casey

103 Lubin's Rural Cot
Returning home across the
plain

105 The Indigent Peasant
Tho the muses neer smile by
the light of the sun

107 The London March

109 My Native Land
My native land I bid adieu

111 Good Morrow to your Night Cap

112 [Blank]

113 [Blank]

74. *RHODE ISLAND: PROVIDENCE. BROWN UNIVERSITY, JOHN HAY LIBRARY,
HARRIS COLLECTION. MUSIC, CA 68E, RARE BOOKS.*

"EUNICE CAREW'S SONG BOOK. JAN'ER 1790." [ii],
86 pp. 20.5 cm.

Blue paper covers; two gatherings (44 and 42 pp.)
loosely sewn through the folds.

Entries in same hand and ink and on same paper.

Inscriptions: "July 10, 1792," front cover;
"January 10, 1792," p. 55; ornamented title-
page (p. [i]).

This MS is one of four music books at this library
copied by Eunice Carew, apparently of Norwich,
Connecticut; see William Dineen, "Early American
Music Books." The title page is reproduced there
opposite p. 56.

Contains 43 secular songs, of which only 11
indicate music. Includes the words to the victory

song beginning "Welcome mighty Chief," and
entitled, "A Sonata, Sung by a Number of Young
Girls, as General Washington Passed under the
Triumphal Arch Raised on the Bridge at Trenton,
April 21st, 1789," p. 18 (set by Reinagle and
published by him in December of that year; see
Sonneck-Upton, pp. 63-64).

Index, p. [ii].

Melody only, unless otherwise indicated.

Page   Page

       Shall I my dear mama tell   78 [Song without music]
       2 parts (2 sopranos or
       soprano and alto); vv.   80 Black Slovin
       1-4 as text.   As I was walking to take
                               the air

75 *Inkle & Yarrico*, Oh, Say   2 parts (treble and bass);
       Simple Maid, a Favorite   vv. 1-5 as text.
       Dialogue to Which is
       Annexed the Original   82 [Blank, with staves in part]
       Song of Oh Say Bonny
       Lass   83 [Blank]
       Oh say simple maid
       Oh say bonny lass   84 [Song without music]
       2 parts (treble and bass);
       vv. 1-4 of each song as
       text. Apparently copied
       from the publication by
       Benjamin Carr (New York,
       ca. 1796; see Sonneck-
       Upton, p. 307).

75. *RHODE ISLAND: PROVIDENCE. BROWN UNIVERSITY, JOHN HAY LIBRARY, HARRIS COLLECTION, MUSIC, M12928M, VOLUME 1, RARE BOOKS, MSS.*

COPYBOOK CONTAINING CHIEFLY VOCAL MUSIC. [19] pp. 16 x 20 cm.

Bound in thin cardboard with decorated paper covers; label on front cover bears name and date, "Sussana Mueller,Nov. 21st 1800."

Entries in same hand and ink and on same paper.

William Dineen, in his "Early American Manuscript Music Books," pp. 58-62, Believes "Sussana Mueller" to be the same as "Susan Miller," compiler of a similar MS cataloged by the John Hay Library as M12928m, volume 2. There both names are subsumed under the entry, "Miller, Susan, comp. [Manuscript music books...]." Dineen also surmises from circumstantial evidence that these MSS had some association with Moravian communities in Pennsylvania. "T[une] 39" below was composed by Christian Gregor, whose tune book was in general use there after 1784. The "Susan Miller" MS is copied on "wove" paper not generally used here before 1800, and its repertory is more germane to the Moravian tradition; therefore it has been excluded from this survey, but an inventory may be found in Dineen's article, p. 62. "T[une] 151" below is reproduced in Dineen's article, opposite p. 56.

Pagination added in pencil.

Page

Page

1 T. 151. How Shall I Meet
   My Saviour

2 Chor. Wär uns das Kindlein
   Treble and bass; includes
   English text usually
   associated with this tune,
   "Life let us cherish."

3 (Tune 14) Jesus Thy Word is
   My Delight
   Treble and bass.

4 T. 39. Das ihn dort im [?]
   Treble and bass; includes
   English translation,
   beginning, "To God our
   Imanuel made flesh."

5 [Blank]

6 The Dying Christian to His
   Soul. A Celebrated Ode
   by Mr. Pope for Three
   Voices.
   Vital sparks of heavenly
   flame
   For soprano, alto, and
   bass, on 3 staves; Alexander Pope is the author
   of the words.

12 Andantino
   As the branches are connected
   Duet for soprano, alto,
   and bass (keyboard).

14 The Sisters, Composed by
   Mr. Hook
   Jane was a woodman's
   daughter
   Treble and bass (keyboard);
   vv. 2-3 as text.

16 Allegretto, Composed by Mr.
   Hook
   How does my lady's garden
   grow
   For soprano, alto, and
   bass on 3 staves.

18 Rosa, Composed by A. Reinagle
   Majestic rose the god of day
   Treble and bass (key-
   board); opening upside-
   down from back cover and
   reading toward center;
   pagination reflects this
   procedure, so that "p. 19"
   appears on the verso of
   p. 17.

76. *VIRGINIA: RESTON. IRVING LOWENS (PRIVATE COLLECTION).**

"CATHARINE AKERLY'S MUSIC BOOK, BETHLE[HEM, PA.],
DEC. 19TH, 1792." [90], [iii] pp. 20 x 26.5 cm.

Title from front flyleaf.

Originally bound in brown leather with gold-
tooled border .5 cm. from edge; only one cover
now remains.

Entries apparently in same hand and ink and
on same paper. Inserted at one end are three
loose leaves of different papers, one bearing

*Lowens moved to Baltimore, Maryland, after this survey went to press.

76. *VIRGINIA: RESTON. IRVING LOWENS (CATHARINE AKERLY)*

watermark with name "Vander Ley" and crest.

Inscriptions: "May 17th, 1794," p. [29]; song text, beginning "What bard, O Time, discover," from *The Duenna* (London, 1775), on back flyleaf.

For voice and keyboard or keyboard solo.

Page [Pagination supplied]

1 Favorite La Chasse by
J. C. Moller

4 Larghetto
He shall feed his flock like
a shepherd

6 Primrose
Come buy of poor Kate
primroses
Vv. 2-3 as text.

7 Malbrouk

8 Queen Mary's Lamentation
I sigh and lament me in vain
Vv. 2-3 as text.

10 Ploughboy
A flaxen headed cow boy
V. 2 as text.

12 Allegro

13 [Untitled]

14 Moderato par Foose
When the rosy morn appearing

15 The Blind Boy
O say what is that thing
call'd light
Vv. 2-5 as text.

16 Gigue

18 Allegro con spirito

21 La Belle Catherine

22 The Nightingale
Sweet nightingale no more
complain

24 Lowland Willy
When o'er the dawns at
early day
Vv. 2-3 as text.

25 Sweet Tyrant Love
Sweet tyrant love

Page [Pagination supplied]

26 Dolly
The sun was sunk beneath
the main
Vv. 2-3 as text.

27 Why Am I Doom'd
Why am I doom'd to spend
my days
Vv. 2-4 as text.

28 Collin and Dolly
The morning cloud was ting'd
with gold
Vv. 2-3 as text.

30 Henry's Cottage Maid. By Pleyel.
Ah! where can fly my souls
true love?
Vv. 2-5 as text.

32 With Lowly Suit & Plain-
tive Ditty
With lowly suit and plain-
tive ditty

35 Pauvre Madelon
Could you to battle march
away
Vv. 2-3 as text.

37 [Untitled]
Where is he? ye feeling
hearts
Vv. 2-3 as text; in C minor
and possibly to be con-
tinued by the following:

38 [Untitled]
Then quit the haunts, where
sorrow dwels
V. 2 as text; in E-flat
major, and possibly a
continuation of the
preceding.

39 The Heavy Hours. Jackson.
The heavy hours are almost

Page [Pagination supplied]   Page [Pagination supplied]

      past
        Vv. 2-3 as text.

40   Three Sweet-hearts, &c.
       Three sweet hearts I boast
       Vv. 2-4 as text.

43   Thy Fatal Shafts &c.
       Thy fatal shafts unerring
       prove
       Vv. 2-3 as text.

44   Fresh & Strong &c.
       Fresh & strong the breeze
       is blowing

45   [Blank]

46   Still the Lark Finds Repose
       Still the lark finds repose

49   The Lamplighter
       I'm jolly Dick, the lamp-
       lighter
       Vv. 2-5 as text.

51   [Blank]

52   La Fayette. A New Song
       As beside his chearful fire
       Vv. 2-7 as text.

54   President's March

55   [Untitled]
       Were I oblig'd to beg
       my bread

56   Could I Bid the Fond Passion
         to Cease. Sung by Mrs.
         Seymour in the Opera,
         Lock & Key
       Could I bid the fond
       passion to cease

58   Musical Medley
       Gentlemen and ladies, could
       I beguile you

62   The Female Cryer. Sung at
         Vaux Hall Gardens
       I've lost my heart

66   Scotch Song: Anna
       Shepherds I have lost
       my love
         V. 2 as text.

68   The Silver Moon
       Where shall I seek the
       lovely swain
         V. 2 as text.

70   The Convent Bell
       When waken'd by the convent
       bell
         V. 2 as text.

72   I'll Die for No Shepherd
         Not I
       When first on the plain I
       began to appear
         Vv. 2-3 as text.

74   Lullaby
       Peaceful slum'bring on the
       ocean
         V. 2 as text.

75   The Contented Cottager
       My Collin is the kindest lad
         Vv. 2-3 as text.

77   Scotch Air
       From thee Eliza I must go
         Vv. 1-2 as text.

78   Since Then I'm Doom'd. Sung
         by Mrs. Marshall in *The
         Spoil'd Child*
       Since then I'm doom'd

80   In Airy Dreams
       In airy dreams soft fancy
       flies
         Vv. 1-4 as text.

82   Snatch Fleeting Pleasures.
         Translated from the German.
       Snatch fleeting pleasures.
         Vv. 2-5 as text.

83   Song in *Bluebeard*

84   My Journey is Love
       When I was at home as the
       lark
         Vv. 2-4 as text.

86   When Pensive I Thought on
         My Love
       When pensive I thought of
       my love
         V. 2 as text.

76. *VIRGINIA: RESTON. IRVING LOWENS (CATHARINE AKERLY)*

Page [Pagination supplied]

88 An Irish Air
      As down on Banna's banks
      Vv. 2-6 as text.

90 [Untitled]

Page [Pagination supplied]

i The Cuckoo
     Now the sun is in the west
     V. 2 as text.

77. *VIRGINIA: RESTON. IRVING LOWENS (PRIVATE COLLECTION).**

Copybook. [67] pp. 32 cm.

Bound in half-leather and marbled paper over
boards; printed form of contract between master
of ship and seamen mounted on front cover. Part
of p. [3] and leaf between pp. [30] and [31]
excised.

Entries in same hand and ink. Paper of two
watermarks: an oval crest containing knight
with sword and shield; and initials, "J & R T."

Inscriptions: "Martha Kennedy," inside front cover;
"Martha Brodie," inside back cover, last page,
and pp. [43], [41], and [40] (reading upside down).

Fingered scales and exercises for the keyboard,
pp. [49]-[50].

Contains unaccompanied songs and vocal duets,
works for keyboard alone, and one duet for
guitar (p. [5]). Even-numbered pages are blank
unless otherwise noted.

Page [Pagination supplied]

1 Drink to Me Only, a
      Favorite Duett
      Drink to me only with
      thine eyes
      2 parts.
   How Sweet in the Woodlands
      How sweet in the woodlands
      1-3 parts; includes
      written-out ornament-
      ation. See also p. [29]
      below.
   Soft Murmers
      Be still soft murmurs
      2 parts.

Page [Pagination supplied]

3 Henry's Cottage Maid
      Ah! where can fly my soul's
      true love
      1-2 parts.
   Oh Say Simple Maid
      Oh say simple maid
      Incomplete; partially
      torn out.

5 O Dear What Can the Matter Be
      O! Dear what can the mat-
      ter be
      1-2 parts.
   A Duett for Two Guitars

---

*Lowens moved to Baltimore, Maryland, after this survey went to press.

Page [Pagination supplied]

7 Sweet Transports Gentle
      Wishes Go
      Sweet transports gentle
   wishes go
         Instrumental introduction.
   Babling Echo

8 [Untitled]
      Musical fragment, and
      penmanship exercise.

9 The Rose
      To a shady retreat
   Down in the Valley
      Down in the valley the
      sun setting clearly

11 Black Ey'd Susan
    The Willow
    Selims Complaint

13 The Cottage on the Moor
    When a Little Merry He
    Will You Come to the Bower

14 Ned of the Hill
       At who is that
          Incomplete.

15 Within a Mile of Edinburgh
    No 'Twas Neither Shape
       Nor Feature

17 Lovely Nancy
       How can you lovely Nancy
          With one variation; a
       second variation is
       indicated by title only.

19 Allegro moderato
       1-2 parts.

21 Life Let Us Cherish
       2 parts.
    Tink a Tink
    [Untitled]
       My mother bids me bind
    my hair
          Incomplete.

23 [Untitled]
       My mother bids me bind
    my hair
          V. 2 as text.

Page [Pagination supplied]

24 I Am Young & I Am Friendless
       I am young & I am
       friendless
    A Fav^t Song in *Inkle & Yarico*
       Oh say simple maid

25 Welch Air in *The Cherokee*
       A shepherd wander'd we
       are told

27 The Swelling Canvass
       The swelling canvass caught
       the breeze
          Vv. 2-3 as text.

28 [Untitled]
       Continuation of "How
       Sweet in the Woodlands,"
       p. [29] below.

29 Favorite Song in *The Spoil'd
    Child*
       I am a brisk young sprightly
    lad
          2 parts.
    How Sweet thro the Woodlands
       How sweet in the woodlands
          1-2 parts, continued on
       p. [28] above. See also
       p. [1] above.

30 No My Love No
       For keyboard (2 treble
       voices and bass).

31 Fishing Duett, Cont^d.
       What is beauty but the bait
          Final verse of song on
       preceding excised leaf
       as text.

32 In Gaudy Courts, Favorite Duet
       in *Rosina*
       In gaudy courts with aching
       hearts
          2 parts.

34 Minuet, Grazioso
    Jigg

37 The Honey Moon
       When Mary first my love
       inspired
          Vv. 1-3 as text.

77. *VIRGINIA: RESTON. IRVING LOWENS (MARTHA KENNEDY/BRODIE)*

Page [Pagination supplied]

39-45 [Blank]

  46   Roanoake Waltz - Mary's
           Favorite
           For keyboard.

Page [Pagination supplied]

  48   Cotton Petticoat, or Touch
           Me Just There

  51   Waltz
      Waltz
           Both for keyboard.

53-67 [Blank]

78. *VIRGINIA: RESTON. IRVING LOWENS (PRIVATE COLLECTION).* *

"GEORGE NEWBERRY BOOK." [42] pp. 9.5 x 16 cm.

Title from last page.

Bound in brown cowhide.

Entries in various hands and inks; only
parts of watermark(s) may be distinguished.

Chiefly in diamond notation, including the
2d title below.

Contains parts for tenor and bass only, principally of sacred music believed by the present
owner to have been in common use in the 1730s
or 1740s. The inventory below includes only the
secular titles.

Page [Pagination supplied]

  23   The Chimes

  35   The Divine Use of Musick
      The Glideing Streams

79. *VIRGINIA: RESTON. IRVING LOWENS (PRIVATE COLLECTION).* *

COPYBOOK CONTAINING MUSIC FOR VOICE AND KEYBOARD,
OR KEYBOARD SOLO. [36] pp. 23 x 29.5 cm.

Single signature rough-sewn into dark blue
paper cover. First leaf lacking; part of first
few titles obliterated by disintegrating or
excised paper.

Entries in several hands: "A," pp. [1]-[5],
[17]-[34; "B," pp. [6]-[10]; "C" (apparently

---

*Lowens moved to Baltimore, Maryland, after this survey went to press.

earlier than "B"), pp. [11]-[16]; "D," p.
[34]; "E"(but possibly continuation of "A"),
pp. [35]-[36]. Different inks; wove paper
throughout.

Inscription: "Ann Nivison," on label pasted
inside front cover.

Includes music by an unidentified composer
to nearly all of William Shield's *Rosina*,
with orchestral instruments indicated in keyboard part (see pp. [18]-[36]).

For voice and keyboard or keyboard solo.

Page [Pagination supplied]

1 Tawny Moor. Sung in *The
     Mountaineers*
     Oh happy tawny moor

2 Ella and Edwin

3 [The Caledonian] Maid
     Oh say have you my Mary
     seen the Caledonian maid

4 Bonny Charley

6 Quick March Play'd at the
     Circus
   [Untitled]
     Little thinks the towns-
     mans wife

7 The Streamlet
     The streamlet that flowd
     V. 2 as text.

8 Soft Is the Zephirs
   Count Wartens**leben**
   The Abbey Bells

9 The Jew
   Lord Macdonalds Reel

10 Look Before You Leap
    The Whimsical Lover

11 Sung by Mrs. Crouch –
      Pleyel
      Tho' pity I cannot deny

12 Sung by Sigra Storace
      Adela: Whither my love ah
      whither art thou gone
        Includes indication for
        2 obligato flutes.

Page [Pagination supplied]

14 Since Then I'm Doom'd. Sung
      by Mrs. Jordan in *The
      Spoiled Child*
      Since then I'm doom'd
      V. 2 as text.

16 Yes Yes
      I am a brisk and sprightly
      lad
        V. 2 as text; from *The
        Spoiled Child.*

17 The Favorite New Federal
      Song Adapted to the
      Presidents March. Written
      by J. Hopkinson
    Hail! Columbia happy land

18 Sweet Transports Gentle Wishes
      Go
      Rosina: Sweet transports
      gentle wishes go

20 When William at Eve
      Phoebe: When William at eve
      meets me down at the stile
      V. 2 as text.

21 Overture to Rosina
      Short score (orchestral
      instruments indicated).

30 Whilst with Village Maids
      Rosina: Whilst with Village
      maids I stray

33 The Morn Returns in Saffron
      Drest
      Rosina: The morn returns

Page [Pagination supplied]   Page [Pagination supplied]

      in saffron drest
      2 treble and bass staves.

36 Song in *Rosina*
      Incomplete (part of
      instrumental intro-
      duction only); 3 staves.

34 Waltz

35 Song in *Rosina*
      Her mouth, which a smile
      Includes indication of
      2 clarinet parts.

80. VIRGINIA: RESTON. IRVING LOWENS (PRIVATE COLLECTION).*

COPYBOOK OF ENOCH PEIRCE. 1 leaf, 2-119 [i.e., 168] pp. 14.5 x 20 cm.

Bound in brown leather over boards. Lacking pp. 21-22, 28-29; pp. 84-85 and 90-91 excised. P. [160] numbered as p. 200.

Entries in various hands: "A," p. 1, even-numbered pp. 2-36 (first two titles only), p. [160], and pp. [162]-[163]; "B," pp. 36 (last title only)-76 and possibly pp. 5, 7, and 9; "C" (one or more hands), pp. 77-[159] and p. [164]. The hymns on pp. 41-54 are interspersed in haste with secular tunes in a later hand. Here the titles are scarcely legible, but the notes are clear. Possibly same paper: partial watermarks reveal parts of a crown and of a crest containing shield.

Inscriptions: "William Swasey, March," p. 8; "The property of Enoch Peirce" and his name several times, p. [168].

The MS contains instrumental music for one or two melody instruments (flute(s) or violin(s)) and bass (keyboard and/or violoncello); secular vocal music (texted) for treble only; and sacred vocal music for three voices (two treble and bass, or two voices with keyboard) or for four voices.

Partial Index, pp. [162]-[164].

Melody only, in treble clef, unless otherwise indicated.

---

*Lowens moved to Baltimore, Maryland, after this survey went to press.

Page [Pagination original, pp.
    1-119; supplied, pp. 120-68]

1[*r*] Lesson by Morelli
      Marsellois Hymn

1[*v*] [Untitled fragment]

2   Indian Philosopher
      Treble and bass.
   White Cockade
   Unhappy Swain
      2 treble parts.

3   [Blank]

4   Indian Warrier
      Treble and bass.
   Enraptur'd Hours
   Over the Moore

5   March by Wilson
      Bass only.
   Whos Afraid
      Bass only.
   Bonaparte March
      Bass only; continued
      on p. 7 below.

6   Ih [i.e., Ah] ca Ira
   Young Widow

7   [Untitled]
      Gigue.
   Bonapartes Grande March
      Continued
      Bass only; continued from
      p. 5 above.
   Astleys Hornpipe
      Bass only. See also
      p. 80 below.

8   The Belles of Newyork
   Le Village

9   Blue Bells of Scotland
      Bass only.
   Bugle Horn
      Bass only.
   Air by Pleyel
      Bass only.

10 Washington's March
   Bordeaux March

11 [Blank]

Page [Pagination original, pp.
    1-119; supplied, pp. 120-68]

12 Cotillion
   Cotillion

13 [Blank]

14 Massachusets March
   Bonny Jean

15 [Blank]

16 Jack Lattin
   Grano's Trumpet Tune

17 [Blank]

18 Air in *Apollo and Daphne*
   Minuet by Mr. Handel
   Dying Swan

19 [Blank]

20 Maurice Franch Minuet
   Shepherds Complaint

23 [Blank]

24 The Agreeable Surprise
   Matelotte Auglaile

25 [Blank]

26 Burdino's Concert

27 [Blank]

30 Lady Washington
   Fresh and Strong
      Fresh and strong the breeze
      is blowing
   Roslin Castle

31 [Blank]

32 York Fuzealears
   The Wanderer
   Come Haste to the Wedding

33 [Blank]

34 How Imperfect is Expression
   The Hermit
   Lady Nancy

35 [Blank]

36 Contented Swain
      O Cupid forever I fear
      not thy quaver

Page [Pagination original, pp. 1–119; supplied, pp. 120–68]

Page [Pagination original, pp. 1–119; supplied, pp. 120–68]

Leander
  Leander on the Bay of
  Hellespont
God Save the King

37 The Primrose Girl
      Incomplete.

38 The Rose Tree

39 Zura. CM. Major
      Salvation, let the glor-
      ious sound
      4 parts.

41 (13) Mo[?]ingo
      See also p. 52 below;
      for bass line see p.
      [139] below.
    Hartley. CM. Minor
      That awful day will
      surely come
      4 parts.

43 Miss Carey (254)
    Suffield. CM. Major
      We bring our mortal pow'rs
      to thee
      4 parts.

44 A Hornpipe

46 Brenton SM. Minor
      Have mercy Lord on me
      2 treble and bass parts.

47 (7) G. D. *40 Thieves*
    Wendell CM. Major
      Awake, awake, my soul
      to praise
      4 parts.

48 (9) C. 2. M.

49 Fenwick. CM. Minor
      On cherub's wings Jehovah
      comes
      4 parts.
    [Untitled fragments]
      Melody only, on last 2
      staves.

51 Temple HM. Major
      Lord of the worlds above
      2 treble and bass parts.

52 Marrgo [?] (13)
      See also p. 41 above; for
      bass line see p. [139]
      below.

53 Urwick. LM. Major
      Thy favor, Lord, surprise
      our souls
      2 treble and bass parts.

54 Major Minor (15)

55 Swanston. Ps. 50th. Dr. Watts
      The Lord, the Sovereign,
      sends his summon forth
      2 treble and bass parts.

57 Silver Street. SM. Smith
      2 treble parts; incomplete.

58 Canada Farewell[?]
      2 treble parts.

59 Lesson 6th
      Incomplete.
    Alburg. Ps. 122d. Dr. Watts
      How pleas'd & bless'd was I
      4 parts.

61 The Day of Rest
      This is the day
      2 treble and bass parts.

65 Eastern. CM. Major
      Lord in the morning
      2 treble and bass parts.

67 Templeton. LM. Major
      When the great Builder
      2 treble and bass parts.

69 Wandsworth. CM. Major
      To thee, before the dawn-
      ing light
      2 treble and bass parts.

70 Blendon. LM.
      Lord when thou dost ascend
      on high
      2 treble and bass parts.

71 Hancock. Hymn 145 Bk 2 Dr.
      Watts. CM. Major
      How sweet and awful
      2 treble and bass parts.

Page [Pagination original, pp.
   1-119; supplied, pp. 120-68]

Page [Pagination original, pp.
   1-119; supplied, pp. 120-68]

 72 Evening Hymn. LM
       My God permit me not to be
       Treble and bass.

 73 Baldwin. CM. Major
       Now to thy heavnly Father's
       praise
       2 treble and bass parts.

 75 Ashholm CM. Major
       2 treble and bass parts.

 76 Turkish Music
     Prelude

 77 Boston Cadets March

 78 March in the Battle of Prague
     The Merry Girls of Newyork

 79 The Zephyr
     Lesson
     Turkish Quick Step - Battle
       of Prague
       See also p. [158] below.

 80 Trip to Nahant
     Quick Step - by Benda
     Astleys Hornpipe
       See also p. 7 above.

 81 The Legacy
     Roving Sailor
     Thimble

 82 Quick Step
     Life Let Us Cherish

 83 Be Gone Dull Care
       2 treble parts.

 86 Yankey Doodle
       See also p. 119 below.
     Serenade
     Boston March

 87 Charley Over the Water
     Chorus of Robbers in the
       Opera of *40 Thieves*
     Felton's Gavot

 88 Gen. Greens March
     Rise Collumbia

 89 Washingtons March
       Partly crossed through;

       see p. 110 below.
     Bonaparte's Grand March
       2 treble parts; pp. 90-
       91 excised before copying.

 93 A Favorite March in The Demo-
       lition of the Bastile
       2 treble parts.

 94 The Battle of the Nile. Adap-
       ted as a March
       2 treble parts.

 95 Bristol March. By O. Shaw
       2 treble parts.

 97 March in *Blue Beard*
       2 treble parts.
     Miss Ash
       2 treble parts.

 99 Grand Spy
       See also p. [158] below.
     Swiss Guard's March
       2 treble parts.

100 For There's No Luck about
       the House
       2 treble parts.

102 Dance in *Tekeli*. A Quick Step
       Only the upper of 2
       treble parts copied.

103 Air in *Blue Beard*
       2 treble parts.

104 French Air
       2 treble parts; not the
       same as that on p.
       [159] below. "Haunted
       Tower" added in pencil.

105 Grand March in *Abaellino*
       2 treble parts.

107 President's March, or, Hail
       Columbia Happy Land
       2 treble parts.

108 The Bugle Horn
       2 treble parts.

[109 Omitted in pagination]

80. *VIRGINIA: RESTON. IRVING LOWENS (ENOCH PEIRCE)*

Page [Pagination original, pp.
     1-119; supplied, pp. 120-68]

110 Washington's March
         2 treble parts; see also
         p. 89 above.

111 Last Week I Took a Wife -
         A Song

112 Fresh & Strong. Air by Handel
         2 treble parts; composed
         by Samuel Arnold (cf.
         Sonneck-Upton, pp. 148-
         49).

113 No. 15
         Only upper of 2 treble
         parts copied.
     Rogues March. No. 18

114 Adam's & Liberty. No. 17
         Only upper of 2 treble
         parts copied.

115 Cork Quick Step
         Only upper of 2 treble
         parts copied.

116 Air by Pleyel
         2 treble parts.

117 Farewell ye Green Fields
         Only upper of 2 treble
         parts copied.
     Sicilian Mariner's Hymn

118 Away with Melancholy (A Glee)
         Only upper of 2 treble
         parts copied.

119 Yankey Doodle 1st
         See also p. 86 above.
     The Russian Dance
         2 treble parts.

120 [Untitled fragments]

122 Sultan Amavath

123 Quick Step

124 Massachusetts March
         2 treble parts.

126 La bella duchessa [?]
     New Jersey

127 Captain Pied's March

Page [Pagination original, pp.
     1-119; supplied, pp. 120-68]

         2 treble parts; incomplete.

128 Fourth Quick March
         2 treble parts.

129 Rural Felicity
         2 treble parts.

130 Sailors Air - A Quick Step
     Grand Dance in *The 40 Thieves*

131 Lord Uxbridge's March
         2 treble parts.

132 The Jubilee [?]
         2 treble parts.
     (6) [Untitled]
         2 treble parts.
     (11) [Untitled]
         2 bass parts.

133 [Untitled]
     (22) [Untitled]
         Bass part only.

134 The Galland Soldier
     Jefferson
     (9) [Untitled]
         Bass part only.

135 Midshipman
     (31) [Untitled]
         Bass part only.

136 Kingsbury Quick Step
         G major; variant of that
         on p. [137] below.
     [Untitled]
     [Illegible title]
         Bass line only.

137 Kingsbury Quick Step
         F major; variant of that
         on p. [136] above.
     No. 1
         Bass line only
     23 [Untitled]
         Bass line only.

138 Spanish Patriots
         Treble and bass parts
         copied consecutively.

139 Maringo [?]
         Bass line only; see also

Page [Pagination original, pp. 1-119; supplied, pp. 120-68]

pp. 41, 52 above.
Miss E. R.

140 Lesson 1st. Unhappy Swain
     2 treble parts.
   Lesson 2nd. German Hymn
     2 treble parts.

141 Lesson 3rd
   Lesson 4th
   Lesson 5th. Friendship
     2 treble parts.

142 Who's Afraid. Or Lesson 6th
     2 treble parts.

143 March by Mr. Wilson. Or
     Lesson [7th]
     2 treble parts.
   Hulls Victory

144 Blue Bells of Scotland
     Only upper of 2 treble
     parts copied.
   March in *Scipio*
     2 treble parts.

146 Sym[phonia]
     For keyboard (treble
     and bass).

148 [Blank]

149 [Blank]

150 [Blank]

Page [Pagination original, pp. 1-119; supplied, pp. 120-68]

151 136th Psalm Tune
   Sherburne
   Maryland

152 [Blank]

153 Lisbon
   Old Hundred
   Dalston
   Hollis

154 Lenox
     Different hand; 2 treble
     parts, of which the 2d
     lacks the final cadence.

155 Lenox
   Russia
   Thirty-Fourth Psalm Tune

156 [Blank]

157 Drink to Me Only
     2 treble parts.

158 Grand Spy. A Quick Step
     Nearly illegible due to
     print-through. See also
     p. 99 above.
   Turkish Quick Step in The
     Battle of Prague
     incomplete. See also p.
     79 above.

159 French Air
     2 treble parts; not the same
     as that on p. 104 above.

160 The Pensive Shepherd
     How gloomy are the fields
     & plain
       Vv. 1-3 as text, p. [161].
       P. [160] numbered as p. 200
       in hand "A."

165-68 [Blank]

---

*81. VIRGINIA: RESTON. IRVING LOWENS (PRIVATE COLLECTION).**

"CLARIONET PRIMO." [iii], 36 [i.e., 96] pp.
10 x 19 cm.

*Lowens moved to Baltimore, Maryland, after this survey went to press.

81. *VIRGINIA: RESTON. IRVING LOWENS (J. WILLIAMS)*

Title from label inside front cover; added title on spine in ink: "PRIMO Clarionet."

Bound in half-leather with marbled paper over boards.

Entries in same hand and ink and on same ruled paper throughout; watermark, visible only pp. [18]-[26], is circle containing eagle.

Inscriptions: "Jno. Williams Jr., July 9, 1799," p. [ii]; "Received New York of John Williams Junr the sum of [remainder blank]," inside back cover.

Pagination begins on verso of p. [iii] and ends on p. 36; first fifty-five entries are numbered in sequence with additional numbers in parentheses for the first thirty-one entries, suggesting that these were selections copied from an as yet unidentified collection.

Melodies for one clarinet, occasionally with part for second clarinet copied on same or opposite page.

Page	[Pagination original, pp. 1-36; supplied, pp. 37-96]	Page	[Pagination original, pp. 1-36; supplied, pp. 37-96]
1	No. 1 (4) Paddy Whack		No. 14 (36) [Untitled]
3	No. 2 (5) H's a Kissing Me		No. 15 (44) Madrigal
4	No. 3 (6) This Bottle's the Sun of Our Table	12	No. 16 (50) Taliho
	No. 4 (7) Kiss My Lady Crossed through in pencil.	13	No. 17 (51) Dead March
			No. 18 (52) Old Robin Gray
	No. 4 Quick Step In pencil.		No. 19 (57) Schomberg's March
5	No. 5 (7) Kiss My Lady	14	No. 20 (61) Rupert's March
	No. 6 (9) [Untitled]	15	No. 21 (62) Care Thou Canker
6	No. 7 (13) Fishers Minuet		No. 22 (63) [Untitled]
	No. 8 (19) Big Bow Vow	16	No. 23 (64) With Early Horn
8	No. 9 (24) [Untitled]	17	No. 24 (67) Sun Flower
9	No. 10 (26) Come Rouse Brothers Sportsmen		No. 25 (68) [Untitled]
		18	No. 26 (72) Wilsons Favourite March
10	No. 11 (31) Dead March	19	No. 27 (80) [Untitled]
	No. 12 (32) Williams's Favourite March		No. 28 (93) [Untitled]
		20	No. 29 (103) [Untitled]
11	No. 13 (33) Minuet La Cour	21	No. 30 (100) Topsail Shivers
			No. 31 (106) [Untitled]

Page [Pagination original, pp.
      1-36; supplied, pp. 37-96]

22 No. 32 Presidents March
    No. 33 Jockey to the Fair

23 No. 34 Aloa House
    No. 35 My Dog and My Gun

24 No. 36 When Rural Lads and
           Lasses Gay
    No. 37 Sinclears Farewell

25 No. 38 Washingtons March
           See also p. 36 below.
    No. 39 Roslin Castle

26 No. 40 Jem of Aberdeen

27 No. 41 March in *Lodoiska*

28 No. 42 Miss Poots Fancy
    No. 43 The Blue Bells of
           Scotland

29 No. 44 Owen
    No. 45 Marionetts Cotillion

30 No. 16 The Fop
    No. 47 Lady Salisburys Whim
    No. 48 Free and Accepted
           Masons

31 No. 49 The Welch Harper
    O'er the Water to Charlye

32 No. 50 The Caledonian Laddy -
           Hook

33 No. 51 Adams and Liberty

34 No. 52 When Pensive I Thought
           on My Love

35 No. 53 Presidents March
    La Belle Catherine

36 No. 54 New German Spa
    No. 55 [crossed through]
           Washingtons March
           See also p. 25 above;
           this melody is an octave
           lower.

37 Handel's Clarionet with the
           Second
           Duet.

38 The Belleisle March

Page [Pagination original, pp.
      1-36; supplied, pp. 37-96]

39 The Dying Indian
           Duet.
    Indian Dance

40 The Soldiers Adieu

41 Caledonian Laddy
           Duet.

43 Le Pipe de Tabac

44 The Pantaloon

45 Marseilles March
           Duet.

47 March in *Matteruma*

48 A Lesson by Morelli

49 March in *Columbus*
           Duet.

51 [Untitled]
           Duet; only primo copied.

53 Lolloboy
           Duet.

55 French Guards March
           Duet.

56 The Vicar and Moses

57 March
           Duet.

59 Allegro
           Duet.

60 Rose Tree
           Duet.

61 Richard Coeur de Lion March
           Duet.

63 March - Henry 4th
           Duet.

65 [March]
           Duet.

66 Federal March
           Duet.
    Scotch Luck

67 Wilsons Favourite
           Duet.

81. *VIRGINIA: RESTON. IRVING LOWENS (J. WILLIAMS)*

Page [Pagination original, pp. 1-36; supplied, pp. 37-96]

69 Gov. Strongs March
71 Holstines March
72 [Blank]
73 Feltons Gavott
      Incomplete.
   Genl. Greens March
      Duet.

74 Printer Boy
   Bonapartes Favourite

Page [Pagination original, pp. 1-36; supplied, pp. 37-96]

75 Greens March
   Short Troop
   17th Regiment

76 Cold Stream
   40th Regiment

77 Steubens March
   [Untitled]

78 Handles Water Piece

79 Handles Clarionet

80-96 [Blank]

82. *VIRGINIA: RESTON. IRVING LOWENS (PRIVATE COLLECTION).* *

COPYBOOK CONTAINING MUSIC PRINCIPALLY FOR FLUTE.
[48] pp. 11 x 23.5 cm.

Bound in quarter-leather and marbled paper over boards. Only pp. 19 and 20 are numbered. Front flyleaf excised, as are five leaves between pp. [26] and [27], and two between pp. [32] and [33].

Entries in one hand through p. [24], but several hands thereafter; same paper throughout.

Inscriptions: "Done April 17," p. 19; "Done April 20," p. 20.

Flute fingering chart, recto of back flyleaf.

Melody only, in treble clef, unless otherwise noted. Includes three duets for clarinet and bassoon, pp. [27]-[30].

Page [Pagination supplied]

1 God Save the King
  O Dear What Can the Matter Be

2 White Cockade
  Jockey to the Fair

3 Pease Upon a Trencher
  Hope Thou Nurse

4 Maggie Lawder with Variations

Page [Pagination supplied]

7 New Lango Lee

8 Marseillois. March

9 Mountaneers

10 The Irish Washerwoman
   A Smile from the Girl of
     My Heart in *The Woodman*

11 Old Fowler

*Lowens moved to Baltimore, Maryland, after this survey went to press.

Page [Pagination supplied] Page [Pagination supplied]

12 O Love What the Deauce Do
    You Want, in *Birds of
    a Feather*

13 Wine Cannot Cure

14 Presidents March

15 The Rose
    Guardian Angels

16 Mrs. Casey

17 Malbrouk

18 [Untitled]
    Fairy Dance

19 Bluebells of Scotland
    Caravan March

20 March in *Bluebeard*
    Salem Air

21 Massachusetts March

22 The March in Prince
    Eugene

23 Quick March in *Cymon*

24 March in *Abelinio*
    Fragment.

25 Unhappy Swain
    Treble and bass;
    untutored hand.

26 [Blank]

27 No. 1
    Duet for clarinet and
    bassoon; each part
    copied on separate page.

29 No. 2
    Duet for clarinet and
    bassoon; each part
    copied separately.

30 No. 3
    Duet for clarinet and
    bassoon; each part
    copied separately.

31 [Blank]

32 Salem Cadets
    Bassoon part only.

33 [Untitled]
    Reading in opposite
    direction.

34 [Blank]

35 [Untitled]
    Scales; reading in oppo-
    site direction.

37 [Blank]

38 [Untitled]
    Much later hand, in pen-
    cil; reading in oppo-
    site direction.

40 [Untitled]
    O Lord thou art my God
    Vocal duet; reading in
    opposite direction.

47 [Blank]

48 [Untitled]
    Secondo only; in pencil.

*83. VIRGINIA: RESTON. IRVING LOWENS (PRIVATE COLLECTION).**

COPYBOOK. [78] pp. 22.5 x 28 cm.

Bound in half-leather and hand-painted paper
over boards; paper stamp on cover, "Property
of [erased]," later covered by orange stamp
and now torn away.

All entries except the last in same hand and

*Lowens moved to Baltimore, Maryland, after this survey went to press.

83. *VIRGINIA: RESTON. IRVING LOWENS (ANON. 2)*

ink and on the same paper throughout.

For voice(s) and keyboard, or keyboard alone.

Page [Pagination supplied]

Page [Pagination supplied]

Page [Pagination supplied]   Page [Pagination supplied]

  75 Old Fowler. Composed by   78 Fresh & Strong
        Mr. Shield   Fresh and strong the
      Bright Chanticlear pro-   breezes blowing
      claims the dawn   Includes fingering for
        Vv. 2-3 as text.   keyboard.

84. VIRGINIA: RESTON. IRVING LOWENS (PRIVATE COLLECTION). *

COPYBOOK CONTAINING SONGS WITH KEYBOARD ACCOM-
PANIMENT AND MUSIC FOR KEYBOARD SOLO. [88] pp.
19.5 x 24.5 cm.

    Bound in brown leather, originally stamped
    with gold tooled border. Page(s) following
    p. [20] apparently excised.

    Entries apparently in same hand, except for
    added text, pp. [84]-[85]. Two different
    papers, both with watermarks bearing crests,
    one with initials "L V G" and the other
    with a *fleur de lis*. Pp. [82]-[87] are copied
    from the opposite direction, and may possibly
    have been entered earliest: the watermarks
    read in this direction, and the price, "2/6,"
    is written inside this front cover.

    Inscriptions: titles on pp. [23], [26], [56],
    [58], [74], and page pinned over p. [76] bear
    dates from 1763 to and including 1766.

Page [Pagination supplied]   Page [Pagination supplied]

  1 [Untitled]   My fond shepherds of late
      Hark, hark, hark her sweet   V. 2 as text.
      voice all plaintive sounds

  2 Lesson by Morelli   10 Lord Howe's Minuet

  3 Lord Bentick's Minuet   12 Song in *Harlequin Invation* by
                           Dr. Boyce
  4 Mrs. Gardiner's Minuet   Come cheer up my lads
      Miss Shepherd's Minuet   Chorus: Heart of oak are
                           our ships; vv. 2-4 as text.
  5 Capt Gambier's Minuet

  6 Mr. O'Bryan's Minuet   14 Gavot by Handel

  7 Mrs. Pitt's Minuet   15 Air in *Harlequin Sorcerer*
                           Ye chearfull virgins have
  8 Song in the Opera of *Eliza*:   ye seen
      Set by Mr. Arne. Sung by
      Sig^a Frasi   17 [Blank]

---

*Lowens moved to Baltimore, Maryland, after this survey went to press.

Page [Pagination supplied]

18 Lesson by Lully

20 Attic Fire in the Opera
      of *Eliza*
      When all the attic fire
      was fled
          Incomplete.

21 The Genoise Minuet

22 Colinet: A Dialogue Sung by
      Mr. Lowe & Mrs. Lampe
      Now the happy knot is ty'd

23 The True Blue Minuet. 1763.

24 A Song in *Artaxerxes*
      Let not rage thy bosom

26 A New Minuet, 1763.

27 A New Minuet, 1763

28 A Hornpipe

30 A Favourite Song in
      Artaxerexes
      In infancy our hopes and
      fears
          Vv. 2-4 as text.

32 [Untitled]
      The echoing horn calls the
      sportsmen abroad

35 A Lesson

36 Allegro

37 Kingsleys [or J. Lings-
      leys?] March

38 A French Country Dance

39 A French Horn Tune

40 [Blank]

41 [Blank]

42 The French Marriens March

44 Mr. Lyttan's Minuet

45 The Bath Figure

46 A Dutch Turks March

47 A Dutch Reavalry

48 The Queens Taptow

49 The Hessian Taptow

Page [Pagination supplied]

50 [Blank]

51 Sr. George Saville's March

52 A Lesson by Morelli

53 Gavota

54 [Untitled]

55 [Untitled]
      Fair Hebe I left with
      cautious design
          See also p. [77] below.

56 A New Song, 1764
      What shepherd or nymph
          Vv. 2-4 as text on sep-
          arate sheet pinned in.

58 A New Minuet, 1765

59 In the Opera of *The Maid of
      the Mill*
      Free from sorrow, free
      from grief
          Pp. [60] and [62] blank;
          continued on separate
          sheet pinned to p. [66]
          below.

64 Garrick Rant

65 [Blank]

66 [Blank]
      See p. [59] above.

67 Sung by Mr. Beard in *The
      maid of the Mill*
      Hark, 'tis I your own
      true lover

72 [Untitled]
      Genteel is my Damon en-
      gaging his air
          Vv. 2-4 as text.

74 A New Minuet, 1765

75 The Queen's [Minuet]

76 [Blank]
      See p. [77] below.

77 [Untitled]
      Fair Hebe I left with a
      cautious design
          Vv. 1-4 as text, entitled

Page [Pagination supplied]   Page [Pagination supplied]

   "Fair Hebe a New Song,   84 [Untitled]
   1766," on separate sheet   Oh Sandy why leavs't thou
   pinned in over p. [76].   thy Nelly to mourn
   See also p. [55] above.   Vv. 2-4 as text, in
                                        later hand.
78 [Untitled]
    When a maid in way of   86 A Song for This New Militia
    marriage first is courted   to a March for Many Instru-
                                     ments   Sung by Lowe: the
80 [Blank]   Words by Lockman: and Set
                                     to Music by Worgan
81 Chaise Marien   Hark this loud drum
    My dearest life were thou   Vv. 2-3 as text.
    my wife
                                  88 [Blank]
82 [Untitled]
    Our glory renown'd on the
    ocean and shore
       Vv. 2-4 as text.

85. VIRGINIA: RESTON.   IRVING LOWENS (PRIVATE COLLECTION).*

PART OF A MUSICAL COPYBOOK.   [44] pp.   30 cm.

   Removed from binding but spine still sewn;
   pages trimmed.

   Entries in same hand and ink and on same paper.

   Inscription: "Copied from a copy taken by T.
   Barton from a music book printed at Philadelphia
   for A. Reinagle [1789; cf. Sonneck-Upton, p.
   212]," p. [38].

   Chiefly music for violin on single staff, some-
   times with song text underlaid.

Page [Pagination supplied]   Page [Pagination supplied]

1 Eheliche Gutenacht -   5 Rondo
   Andante moderato   Bottom of pp. [7]-[8]
   Gute Nacht! gute Nacht!   torn away.
      For voice and keyboard
      on 2 staves; vv. 2-6   8 Ganz war ich
      as text.   For keyboard.

2 Langsam und ausdrucksvoll   9 Maria Stern
      Vergiss mein nicht   [Untitled]
      For voice and keyboard on   Stay sweet enchanter of the
      3 staves; vv. 2-3 as text.   grove
                                       For voice and violin ob-

*Lowens moved to Baltimore, Maryland, after this survey went to press.

85. *VIRGINIA: RESTON.   IRVING LOWENS   (ANON. 4)*

Page [Pagination supplied]   Page [Pagination supplied]

42 Damon & Clora: a Duet   44 [3 illegible titles]
  Primo (Clora): Go false   In German script.
  Damon, go   Three Sweethearts I Have
  Secondo (Damon): Turn
  fair Clora turn

WORKS CITED

Breton, Arthur J. *Guide to the Manuscript Collections of the New York Historical Society*. Westport, Conn.: Greenwood Press, 1972.

The British-Union Catalogue of Early Music Printed before the Year 1801. London: Butterworths Scientific Publications, 1957.

Britton, Allen P.; Lowens, Irving; Crawford, Richard. *Sacred Music in America through 1810*. Worcester, Mass.: American Antiquarian Society, forthcoming.

Compleat Instruction for the German Flute. London: J. Bland, [178-?].

The Compleat Tutor for the German Flute. London: Chas. & Saml. Thompson, [1775].

Custis, George Washington Parke. *Recollections and Private Memoirs of Washington by His Adopted Son*. New York: Derby & Jackson, 1860.

Dictionary of American Biography. New York: C. Scribner's Sons, 1928-.

Dineen, William. "Early American Music Manuscript Books." *The Musical Quarterly* 30(1944):50-62.

Entire New and Compleat Instructions for the Fife, Containing the Best and Easiest Directions to Learn That Instrument with a Collection of the Most Celebrated Marches, Airs, &c. Performed in the Guards & Other Regiments. London: Longman and Broderip, n.d.

Fiske, Roger. *English Theatre Music in the Eighteenth Century*. London: Oxford University Press, 1973.

The Flute Master Compleat Improv'd ... Book the First. Corrected edition. London: John Young, 1706.

Frankenstein, Alfred. *William Sidney Mount*. New York: Abrams, 1975.

Gombosi, Marilyn Purnell. *Catalog of the Johannes Herbst Collection*. Chapel Hill: University of North Carolina Press, 1970.

The Johannes Herbst Collection. New York: University Music Editions, 1978.

Keller, Kate Van Winkle, and Rabson, Carolyn. *The National Tune Index, Phase 1: 18th Century Secular*. New York: University Music Editions, forthcoming.

Krohn, Ernest C. "Alexander Reinagle as Sonatist." *The Musical Quarterly* 18(1932):143-49.

Lawrence, Vera Brodsky. "Micah Hawkins, the Pied Piper of Catherine Slip, *New York Historical Society Quarterly* 62(1978): 138-65.

Lowens, Irving. *Bibliography of Songsters Printed in America before 1821*. Worcester, Mass.: American Antiquarian Society, 1976.

Muller, Joseph. *The Star Spangled Banner*. New York, 1935. Reprint, New York: Da Capo, 1973.

Musical Journal for the Pianoforte [4(1802-3)].

Parker, John R. *Musical Biography: or Sketches of the Lives and Writings of Eminent Musical Characters*. Boston, 1825. Reprint. Detroit: Information Coordinators, 1975.

Reinagle, Alexander. *The Philadelphia Sonatas*. Edited by Robert Hopkins. Recent Researches in American Music, vol. 5. Madison, Wisc.: A-R Editions, 1978.

_____. *A Selection of the Most Favorite Scots Tunes with Variations for the Piano forte or Harpsichord*. Philadelphia: Printed for the Author, [1787].

Shifflet, Anne Louise. "Church Music and Musical Life in Frederick, Maryland, 1745-1845." Master's thesis, The American University, 1971.

Sonneck, Oscar G. T. *A Bibliography of Early Secular American Music*. Washington: Library of Congress, 1905.

_____. _____. Revised and enlarged by William Treat Upton. Washington: The Library of Congress, Music Division, 1945. Reprint. New York: Da Capo Press, 1964.

_____. *Francis Hopkinson and James Lyon*. Washington, 1905. Reprint. New York: Da Capo, 1969.

_____. "Francis Hopkinson: The First American Poet-Composer and Our Musical Life in Colonial Times." In *Church Music and Musical Life in Pennsylvania in the Eighteenth Century*, edited by William Lichtenwanger. Philadelphia: Pennsylvania Society of the Colonial Dames of America, 1947.

_____. *Report on "The Star-Spangled Banner," "Hail Columbia," "America," and "Yankee Doodle."* Washington, 1909. Reprint. New York: Da Capo, 1972.

Tawa, Nicholas E. "Secular Music in the Late Eighteenth-Century American Home." *The Musical Quarterly* 61(1975):512-14.

Tollefson, Carl. "The Ink Path of the Great: Some Thoughts of an Autograph Collector." *Musical Courier* 109(3 Nov. 1934):6.

Van Cleef, Joy, and Keller, Kate Van Winkle. "The Dance and Its Music in Early New England." In *Early Music in Massachusetts*. Boston: The Colonial Society of Massachusetts, forthcoming.

Wolfe, Richard J. *Secular Music in America 1801-1825*. New York: The New York Public Library, 1964.

INDEX

INDEX

Here in one word-by-word alphabet are titles, first lines, subjects, musical forms, and geographical and personal names. No attempt has been made to supply information not found in the description of the manuscripts themselves. Furthermore, we did not determine which composer was intended by the simple reference in a manuscript to a surname (e.g., Stamitz), although we did supply first names of well-known composers (e.g., Handel, Mozart) when there was no doubt. Under musical forms reference has been given to a particular title only when the manuscript has specified the term indexed. For example, "Columbia" was a well-known patriotic song and appears four times in the index under that title, but under the musical form "COUNTRY DANCES" only once, when the manuscript compiler included the phrase, "Country dance," in the title. To have cited all references to "Columbia" here would have been misleading. Similarly there are many other tunes which are in fact country dances, cited by title only, which do not appear under the heading "COUNTRY DANCES."

The problem of indexing the variant spellings and titles common in the 18th century was a difficult one to resolve, and our solutions are certainly arguable. On the one hand a certain amount of standardization is desirable in order both to bring together what are intended to be the same words, and also to save space. This is within the 18th-century spirit of not being unduly concerned with such trifling inconsistencies. On the other hand, to have standardized all spellings into their 20th-century mold would have destroyed the character of these documents, and, particularly in the case of dance music ("gig," "gigue," "jigg," etc.), perhaps obliterated an overview of valuable evidence as to the ethnic and national sources of this music. We have therefore modified some spellings and made cross-references when some relationship seemed apparent between alphabetically distant titles. Abbreviated words have been interfiled with their complete versions. Under the term "DRAMATIC MUSIC" we have used spellings of titles as cited in Sonneck-Upton, BUC, and Wolfe to save space and to facilitate locating the various excerpts.

No distinction has been made between titles and first lines, which are enclosed in quotation marks, because they often appear interchangeably in the manuscripts themselves.

Subjects and musical forms appear in capitals. Each citation
refers the reader to manuscript and page numbers, separated
by a colon: e.g., 77:25 is a reference to MS No. 77, and
thence to page 25 within that manuscript. (Running manuscript numbers will be found as side heads in the upper
margin of the inventories.) In the title and first line
entries a mnemonic code distinguishes citations of entries
having music alone ("m"), music and song-text ("mw"),
or song-text alone ("w"). Thus under "The complaint,"
the reader may locate the music in MS No. 37, the song-
text in MS No. 41 (p. 97), and both in MSS No. 9 and
41 (p. 121).

   Finally the reader must be cautioned against using
this index to verify the 18th-century provenance of the
musical works cited therein, because the manuscripts indexed
do include entries of a later date.

INDEX

"Alas the battals lost and won,"
   mw 35:33
"Alass poor Cate," m 14:70,
   14:Jr
Albany, N. Y., 32
"Albina," m 5:6
Albrecht, Otto E., 67
"Alburg. PS. 122d," mw 80:59
"Aldridge's allemand," m 5:127
"The ale wife & her barrel,"
   m 14:46
Aleseander's feast, "Air," mw 9:86
Alexandria, Va., 14:145
"Alexandria volunteers march,"
   m 14:145
"Alexis," mw 9:46
"Alknosnok," mw 52:1
"All around the Maypole," m 41:7
"All hail the power of Jesus name,"
   mw 6:62
"All in the downs the fleet was
   moor'd," mw 35:12
"All my past life," m 3:7
"The all of life," mw 4:133
"The all of life is love," m 46:16
"All the day," m 47:inside front
   cover
"Allamande," m 49:56
"Allamando," m 32:19, 58:25
"Allamon," m 32:18
"Allegro by the King of Prussia,"
   m 18:393, 18:394
"Allegro for the organ," m 18:379
"Allemand Swesser," m 5:7
"Allemande," m 5:64, 18:405,
   19:166, 45:61, 49:62,
   55:110, 83:14
"Allemande franedue," m 14:61
"Allemande Swesser," m 5:7
"Allemande Swiss," m 2:52, 14:29,
   45:52
ALLEMANDES (in titles)
   "Aldridge's," 5:127
   "by Cyrowetz," 49:62
   "A favorite," 49:62
   "A favourite," 14:173
   "French," 5:8
   "Shingley's," 47:16
   "Slingsby's," 14:29, 32:20
Allen, General, 37:29
Allen, Mary, 4
Allen, Wilkes, Rev., 4

"Alles kommt zu seinem Ende,"
   mw 31:15
"Alliance," m 14:45
"Allmon Swiss," m 2:52
"Alloa house," m 14:174, 45:78,
   81:23, 85:33; mw 17:32
"Alpha," mw 6:65
"Already see the daughters of the
   land," mw 4:41
"Altho' heav'ns good pleasure,"
   mw 59:6
Ambrose, John, 83
"Amelia," m 1:111
"America," m 13:52
"America commers and freedom,"
   mw 73:75
American Antiquarian Society,
   27-28
"American march," m 52:47
American Museum, 48
American University, 18
"The American's favourite quick
   step," m 2:41
"Amesbury," mw 4:34
"Amidst the illusions that oe'r the
   mind flutter," mw 10:175
"Aminta," mw 9:174
"L'amour a mille tourmento,"
   mw 9:42
"An the kirk wad let me be,"
   m 5:57
"An thou wert my ain thing,"
   m 85:32
"Anacreon in heaven (Anacreontic
   song)," m 11:30
Ancram, Lord, 1:80, 5:93
"And can I in sorrow lay down,"
   mw 4:43
"And did you not hear of a jolly
   young waterman," m 3:27
"Andre," mw 4:70
Andre, Major John, 4:59, 4:90,
   41:36, 53:19; biographical
   note, 47:73
"André's complaint," mw 41:36 (1st
   line only). *See also* "Major
   André's complaint;" "A song of
   Major Andrea"
"Andrew Cary," m 2:44, 5:68, 37:14
"Andrew, Saint," 34:167
"Angl:," m 58:13
Ann Arbor, Mich., 29-30

"Anna," m 14:H*r*, 41:15;
  mw 76:66
"Anna, that beautiful maid,"
  mw 73:59
"Anna, the fear," m 17:43
"Anna's lute," mw 16:30
"Anna's urn," m 17:40, 32:2
"Anson's voyage," m 5:11
"The Anspach march," m 18:148
"The answer," mw 22:3
"An anthem from the 114th psalm,"
  mw 9:180
ANTHEMS, 9:157, 9:176, 9:180,
  15:28*v*
Antrim, Lord, 14:114, 14:D*r*
"Apollo," m 3:25; mw 4:11; original
  copybook title, 4
Apollo and Daphne, "Air," 80:18;
  "Tune," m 47:1.
"Apollo turned sheperd," m 52:55
"Apples for ladies," m 13:88
"Arabella," w 4:144*v*
"Are you sure the news is true,"
  mw 4:17
"Aria," m 18:227, 19:128, 58:3,
  58:11, 58:17, 58:21
"Aria andante," mw 9:53
"Aria del Signor Adolfo Hasse,"
  mw 56:28
"Aria francese," m 9:18
Ariadne, "Air," m 5:84, 67:20;
  "Minuet," m 18:368
ARIAS, 9
"Arietta," mw 83:72
"Arietta veneziana," mw 10:184
"Ariette," m 83:14; mw 55:123
"Ariette italiana," m 1:20
"Arioso," m 18:227, 19:142
"Arise, arise Britainnia's sons
  arise," mw 15:6*v* (textual 1st
  line only), 18:160
"L'armadilla," m 58:68
"Armonica domestica," 54
Arne, Thomas Augustine, 1:106–107,
  4:43, 9:112, 9:134, 9:146,
  47:76, 50:16, 84:8
"Arnoe's vale," mw 9:95
Arnold Samuel, 35:29, 80:112
Artaxerxes, "In infancy our hopes
  and fears," mw 84:30;
  "Let not rage thy bosom,"
  mw 84:24

"As beside his chearful fire,"
  mw 76:52
"As bringing home," m 47:29
"As Celia was learning on a spinnet
  to play," mw 37:54
"As Cupid in the garden stray'd,"
  mw 22:17
"As down on Bana's banks I stray'd,"
  mw 21:66. *See also* "Banks of Banna"
"As down on Banna's banks," mw 76:88
"As I walked fresh one morning in
  May," m 37:35
"As I was going to Baltimore,"
  m 13:83
"As I was going to Negro Hill,"
  m 13:81
"As I was walking to take the air,"
  mw 4:68, 74:80
"As in the blooming spring," mw 9:58
"As now my bloom," m 47:61
"As porter Will along St. Paul's
  did move," mw 9:66
"As Roger was driving his wagon one
  day," m 2:24
"As the branches are connected,"
  mw 75:12
"As thro' the grove," m 5:70
"As tink'ring Tom thro' streets his
  trade did cry," mw 9:69
"Ashholm," m 80:75
"Asian camp," m 5:53
"The assignation," mw 30:3
Assheton, Susan, 41
"Astley's hornpipe," m 80:7, 80:80
"Astley's ride," m 14:144(2)
"At leangth too soon dear creature,"
  mw 4:70
"At lying down," mw 4:43
"At setting day and rising morn,"
  mw 9:137
"At the close of the day when the
  hamlet was still," mw 4:21, 22:11,
  73:51, 74:6
"At the peaceful midnight hour,"
  mw 35:1
"At this unwanted hour," mw 6:64
"At who is that," mw 77:14
Atalanta, "Air," mw 9:84
Athol, Duchess of, 14:42
The Athradates, "March," m 14:100
"Attic fire," mw 9:170, 84:20
"The attorney," m 14:6

"Before I was married," m 11:31
"Before Jehovah's awful throne,"
    mw 15:24r, 55:33
"Begone dull care," m 80:83;
    mw 55:138, 83:9
"Behind the bush," m 5:151, 37:38
"Behold as the shepherds were
    guarding their sheep," mw 22:10
"Behold the sweet flow'rs around,"
    mw 9:102
"Bekränzt mit Laub den liebvollen
    Becher," mw 31:31
"A belater bridge," m 14:41
"The Belfast voluntiers," m 14:50
"Belile's march," m 18:16. *See also*
    "Belisle's march;" "Belleisle
    march;" "Bellisle march"
"Belisle's march," m 52:20;
    mw 4:86. *See also* "Belile's
    march;" "Belleisle march;"
    "Bellisle march"
"Belknap's march," m 13:55
"La bella duchess," m 80:126
Bellamy Band, 6
Bellamy, Colonel, 6, 6:20
"La belle Catherine," m 3:3, 5:158,
    15:4r, 18:26, 21:77, 46:68,
    58:22, 58:44, 76:21, 81:35, 85:25
"Belleisle march," m 27:23, 41:26,
    81:38. *See also* "Belile's
    march;" "Belisle's march;"
    "Bellisle march"
"The belles of Newyork," m 80:8.
    See also "The merry girls
    of Newyork"
"Bellisle march," m 5:1, 11:22,
    17:24, 20:9, 48:4. *See also*
    "Belile's march;" "Belisle's
    march;" "Belleisle march"
"The bells of Newport," m 11:20
"The bells of Norwich," m 13:21
"The bells of Scotland," m 51:45
Belstead (composer), 3:34
Belville (singer or composer),
    50:52
Benda (composer), 80:80
"Beneath a green shade," m 14:177
"Beneath a weeping willow shade,"
    mw 85:41
"Benevolent Tar," mw 53:20, 73:3
"Bennet's reel," m 14:78

Bentinck, William Henry Cavendish,
    48:38, 84:3
"Berg's minuet," m 5:85
"Bestile soft murmurs of each burl-
    ing rile," mw 58:27
Bethlehem, Pa., 76
"Bettina femo pace," mw 9:20
"Betty Land," m 5:20
"Between the sheets," m 14:132
"Big bow vow," m 81:6
"Billy's jig," m 5:41
BINDINGS, CLOTH, 18; LEATHER, 1, 2,
    4-5, 9-15, 17, 20-22, 27, 30,
    37, 44-45, 48-49, 54-57, 67,
    76-84; PAPER, 3, 16, 19, 23-25,
    31, 43, 58, 73-75, 79, 83;
    PAPER (MARBLED), 1, 4, 9-12, 15,
    21-22, 54-56, 77, 82
"The bird of the rose," m 46:34
"The bird that hears," m 47:26
"The bird that hears her nestlings
    cry," mw 14:113
"Birds in the aire," m 47:inside front
    cover
Birds of a feather, "O love what
    the deauce do you want," m 82:12
"The birks of Abergeldie," m 14:150
"The birks of Endermay," m 5:155; mw 41:127
"The birks of Invermay," m 85:29
"The black bird," m 4:119, 13:27,
    14:26, 17:15; mw 56:40
"Black dance," 5:62, 13:93, 58:33
"Black dancree," m 45:70
"Black-eyed Susan," m 37:44, 77:11;
    mw 35:12
"The black forest," m 58:69
"The black joke," m 5:38, 11:13,
    14:25, 47:47
"Black Marys," m 37:9
"Black Marys hornpipe," m 11:8
"The black sloven," m 2:23, 5:51,
    11:36, 13:7, 37:25; mw 4:68,
    74:80
"The black wall nut," m 14:83
Blac[k]burn, Miss, 14:142
Blackney, General, 47:71
Blair, Mrs., 11:14
Blaise et Babet, [Tune in], m 52:49
Blake, Miss, 2:31
Blanc, Mr., 14:133, 47:73
Blank, Mr., 47:25

Boynwater, m 2:52, 5:55. *See also* "The boin water;" "The buoying water"

"Braes of Aughtertire," m 14:53

"Braes of Ballendean," m 85:32

Braham, John, 15:28*r*, 15:39*v*

"A brandy & wine," m 2:23

"The brave Yanco boys," m 14:57

"Brenton," mw 80:46

"The brick maker," m 5:27, 37:6, 47:4

"Bricklayer," m 17:45

"The briefe meeting," m 14:61

"Bright chanticlear proclaims the dawn," mw 83:75

"Bright Phoebus," m 3:10

"Bright Phoebus has mounted the chariot of day," mw 4:99, 32:6, 32:24

"Bright Sol at length by theater woods," mw 4:76

Brighton, Miss Douglas, 14:19

"Bring flowers, young flowers," mw 61

"The brisk widdow," m 14:91

"Brisk young drummer," m 17:5

Bristol Academy, Taunton, Mass., 23

"Bristol march," m 15:25*v*, 80:95

"Britannia's invitation," m 5:143

"The British grenadier," 4:51 (title only); m 11:40; mw 24:62

"The British grenadiers," m 5:42, 13:82, 20:16, 21:71, 37:52

"The British grenadiers march," m 13:31, 13:106

"The British hero," mw 25:27. *See also* "The hero"

"British muse," m 52:17; w 4:33

"Britons strike home," m 5:121, 47:11

Broadhurst, Miss D., 34, 50:1

Brodie, Martha, 77

Brooklyn, N. Y., 33

"The broom," mw 41:38 (1st line only)

"The broom of Cowdenknows," m 14:134, 17:5

Brown, B. (composer), 4:13, 4:72, 4:91, 4:93

Brown, Captain, 4:128

Brown, Nancy, 53

Brown University, 73-75

Bruce, Lady, 13:87

"Bruce's address to his army," mw 15:41*v*

Brumswick, Dutchess of, 2:51

"Brunswick," mw 18:304

Buche, Mr., 37:5

"The buff coat," mw 11:28

"The bugle horn," m 13:109, 48:1, 80:9, 80:108

"Bugle horn quick step," m 48:29

"Bumble Jack," m 37:22

"Bung your eye," m 11:9

"Bunker Hill," m 11:21, 13:57; mw 15:2*r*, 22:8

Buonaparte. *See* Napolean Bonaparte

"Buonaparte's grand march," m 1:79, 6:50. *See also* "Bonaparte's grand march"

"Buonaparte's march," m 1:19, 18:329. *See also* "Bonaparte's march"

"The buoying water," m 37:26. *See also* "The boin water;" "Boynwater"

"Burbank's march," m 13:112, 51:41

"Burdino's concert," m 80:26

"Burford races," m 5:61

"Burgomasters march," m 1:84

Burgoyne, John, Gen., 1:83

"Burk Thumoth's minuet," m 47:38

"The burletta of *Midas*," m 3:18

"The burn cary," m 14:38

Burrows, Colonel, 55:110

"Bustle and stir in my shop," mw 31:9

"Busy curious thirsty fly," m 37:30

"The butterfly," mw 4:14

"Buttonhole," m 13:17

"By the side of a stream," mw 4:79

"By this fountain's flowery side," mw 50:52

Byrne, Ellen Ann Maria, 73

Byrne, Patrick, 73

"Byrne's fancy," m 73:80

"Ca ira," m 11:9, 83:14. *See also* "Ah ca ira"

"Cacina," m 5:8

"Cackling of the hens," m 5:67

"The Caledonian hunt," m 15:36*r*
"The Caledonian laddy," m 81:32,
    81:41
"The Caledonian maid," mw 10:197,
    73:73, 79:3
"Caledonian reel," m 73:1
Cambell, Colonel, 14:25
"Cambridge," m 21:46
Cambridge (England or Mass.?),
    5:36
"Cameron has got his wife again,"
    m 14:41
"Cameron's frolick," m 14:45
"Campbell's frolick," m 5:56
"Canada farewell," m 14:73, 27:24,
    37:24, 48:7, 80:58
"Canadian volunteers," 48 [lacking]
"Cantata," mw 9:58, 9:67-71, 9:112,
    9:164
"Canzonet by Storace," mw 7:2
CANZONETS (CANZONETTS), 7:1, 10:216
"La capricieuse," m 8:28
"Capt. Blodget's march," m 60:1
"Capt. Blomberg's march," m 14:99
"Capt. Brown's march," m 4:128
"Captain Clark's quickstep,"
    m 2:10
"Capt. Cook country dance," m 14:145
"Capt. Francis Wemyss delight,"
    m 14:62
"Capt. Francis Wemyss strathpey,"
    m 14:61
"Capt. Gambier's minuet," m 84:5
"Capt. Gordon's quick step of the
    36th," m 2:12
"Capt. Houghton's march," m 14:107
"Capt. Johnson's billiard table,"
    m 14:92
"Capt. Kid," m 37:33
"Capt. Lam's minuet," m 14:176
"Capt. McIntosh's reel," m 14:43
"Captain McKay's fancy," m 14:6
"Capt. Mackintosh's fancy," m 3:3
"Cap'n Makintosh's," m 4:124
"Cap. O. Blunder," mw 4:24
"Capt. O'Bosvil's march," m 14:63
"The captain of love," w 47:66
"Captain Pied's march," m 80:127
"Capt. Read's march," m 2:14
    [lacking], 11:8, 14:107
"Capt. Reed's march," m 13:8. *See
    also* "Reed's march"

"Capt. Sargent's quickmarch," m 49:68
"Captain Strong," m 5:47
"Capt. Triumphant," m 14:77
"Captivity," mw 35:44
"Caravan march," m 82:19
"Caravane's march," m 15:17*v*
"Care thou canker of our joys,"
    m 1:23, 14:59, 81:15; 30:22 [lacking]
"Careless Sally," m 11:2, 14:72
Carew, Eunice, 74
"Carlen is your daughter ready,"
    m 11:39
Carmathin, Earl of, 47:80
"Carnawainshires march," m 47:81
Carr, Benjamin, 7, 8, 34, 35, 35:46-
    51, 36, 54, 54:4, 54:16-21, 55,
    55:2-11, 56-60, 62-65, 74:75
Carr, Joseph, 56:1
Carr, William Thomas, Penn[in]g[ton?],
    56:1
Carroll, John, 14
"Carroll's defeat," m 14:31
"Carroll's fancy," m 14:31
"Carroll's fireside," 20, m 14:31
"Carroll's frolick," m 14:31
"Carroll's maggot," m 14:31
"Carroll's thoughts on eternity,"
    m 14:31
"Carroll's 2 of April," m 14:32
"Carroll's whim," m 14:31
Carter, Maria, 10
"The cassano," m 47:79
"Cast my love," m 5:120
"Cast my love thine eyes around,"
    m 47:37; mw 5:108, 9:109
"Castle Berry," m 5:144
Castle of Andalusia, "Flow thou
    regal purple stream," mw 85:14;
    "If I my heart surrender," mw
    55:23
"Catch, for 3 voices," mw 30:7, 30:13,
    30:17, 30:21, 30:39
"Catch, for 4 voices," mw 30:9,
    30:27-28
CATCHES, 30, 37:55
"Catches & glies," m 58:35
"Cate & Davy," m 14:51
Cathcart, Lady, 37:21
"Catherine Ogee," m 14:111
Catskill, N. Y., 48
"Caty's a beauty," m 14:97
"Catys ramble," m 13:77

"Cease a while ye winds to blow,"
   mw 4:5
"Cease your music gentle swains,"
   mw 50:36
"Celebrated air in *The haunted
   tower*," m 1:7
"The celebrated chaccone," m 55:12
"Celebrated movement of Haydn,"
   m 1:8
"The celebrated slow movt in
   Pleyels concerte," m 11:36
"Celebrate this festival,"
   mw 9:204
"The chace," m 46:16. *See also*
   "The chase"
"Chain cotillion," m 4:18, 21:73,
   45:72
"Chaise Marien," mw 84:81
"Chaises retreat," m 11:4
"Chalk's hornpipe," m 45:3
"The challenge," m 13:45
"Chanson francese," mw 9:42
"Chaptico races," m 14:131
"The charge is prepared,"
   m 14:135
"Charleroy," m 1:76
Charleston, S. C., 30, 34
"Charley Bumbo," m 13:34
"Charley over the water," m 13:38,
   13:40, 80:87
"Charlotte McCarthy," m 17:29
"Charming Clorinda evry note you
   breathe," mw 35:16
"Charming cuckoo, bird of spring,"
   mw 50:66
"Charming fair," m 37:1
"The charming fellow," m 14:41
"The charming lover," m 37:30
"Charming Phillis," m 5:79,
   47:11
"Charming village maid," m 3:12
"The chase," m 58:63. *See also*
   "The chace"
"Chaste Dianna," m 14:24
"Chatham," mw 53:30
"Chaucer's recantation,"
   mw 9:120
"Chaunt civvige," m 14:Hr
"Che' b[?]anze vous," mw 46:68
   (1st line only)
"The cheat," m 15:44v, 48:3

"Cheering rosary," m 14:170,
   15:2v
"Chelmsford races," m 14:28
The Cherokee, "Welch air," mw 77:25
"The Cherokee chief," mw 74:64
Cheshire, Conn., 1
"Chesterfield," m 6:66
"Cheti gio vaora fille," mw 9:19
"Chevy Chace," m 5:24, 37:47
"Chi mai cirai, che in questi rozzi,"
   mw 55:15
Chicago, Ill., 14-17
Child, Lewis, 47
"Child of the summer, charming rose,"
   mw 4:50
"Children of the heav'nly King,"
   mw 18:305
CHILDREN'S SONGS, 7:5-11
"Chiling O Guiry," m 20:6, 47:9
"Chimes," m 5:66, 78:23
"China," m 15:23v
"Chloe yeild'd on the morrow sighing,"
   mw 30:31
"Choice of Harlequin," m 14:13
"La chontille cotillion," m 49:6
"Chorus by Rolle," mw 32:15
"Chorus jigg," m 3:24, 13:30, 13:52,
   21:76
"Chorus of robbers in...*40 thieves*,"
   m 80:87
CHORUSES (SAB), 75:6, 75:16. *See
   also* TRIOS, VOCAL
CHORUSES (SATB), 9:172, 15:28v, 26,
   43:17, 83:5. *See also*
   QUARTETS, VOCAL
"Christmas hymn del. Signr.
   Palma," mw 9:125
CHRISTMAS MUSIC, 1:5, 6:64, 9:125,
   22:10, 32:8, 37:34, 53:42
"Christmas ode," mw 6:64
"Ciara," m 17:14
"Circus," m 5:48
CIRCUS MUSIC, 79:6
"Citty's reel," m 14:44
"City dance," m 47:17
CLARINET, 1:2, 4:83, 5:31, 17:16,
   19:168, 49:58, 81:37, 81:79;
   INSTRUCTIONS FOR, 27
CLARINET AND BASSOON MUSIC, 82
CLARINET MUSIC, 27[?], 81; 2 CLAR-
   INETS, 17:16, 81
"Clarionet march," m 6:23

"The convent bell," mw 76:70
"The convention," m 13:111
Cook, Captain 14:145
"Copenhagen waltz," m 52:3
Copp, Beltone, 22
Copp, Jonathan Shipley, 22
"The coral he came over the
  croft," m 14:38
Corelli, Arcangelo, 1:21, 8:9,
  18:404-5, 18:414, 18:419,
  85:24
Cork (Ireland), 37:18, 80:115
"Cork quick step," m 80:115
"The corn planter," m 3:23,
  13:46, 14:60
"Corn riggs," m 47:77; mw 73:61
Corning, Bly, 31
Cornwallis, Lord, 1:32, 14:117,
  18:105
"The coronach," mw 15:21v
"Coronation," mw 6:62
"Coronation march," m 13:109
"The corporal," m 11:37
"Corporal Casey," m 13:108a
Corri, Domenico, 18:152
La Cosarar, "Recitative & air,"
  mw 55:15
"Cotalin trail," m 14:177
"Coteree," m 18:29, 18:328
"Cotillion," m 4:10, 11:35, 18:13,
  18:420, 19:141, 37:13, 41:4,
  41:25, 45:54, 45:59, 48:34,
  80:12 (2); mw 13:64
COTILLIONS (in titles)
  "Alliance," 14:45
  "Chain," 4:18, 21:73, 45:72
  "La chontille," 49:6
  "La Constance," 14:59
  "La damoiselle," 18:134, 19:24
  "Duke of Conflans," 5:58
  "Duke of York's," 48:36
  "Fitz Jame's," 17:29
  "Fly," 5:4
  "A French," 15:17v, 18:134,
    19:24
  "The Gesuit," 45:62
  "Little wood," 14:60
  "A march in the waltz," 48:30
  "Marionets," 3:14, 14:30,
    43:17, 81:29
  "Minnuett," 46:62, 73:66

COTILLIONS (in titles) (*continued*)
  "L'oiseau royal," 45:11
  "Paddy Carey," 15:27r
  "The Pantheon," 14:30, 18:25,
    47:21, 48:21
  "Placide's," 3:22
  "La promenade de St. Cloud," 41:24
"The cottage in the grove," mw 10:194
"Cottage maid," m 49:20
"The cottage on the moor," m 77:13
"The cottages," m 17:43
"Cotton petticoat," m 77:48
"Could I bid the fond passion to
  cease," mw 76:56
"Could you to battle march away,"
  mw 32:34, 76:35
"Count Saxes march," m 47:3
"Count Wartensleben," m 79:8
"Countess of Coventry's minuet,"
  m 45:9
"The country bumkins," m 5:11
"Country dance," m 5:59, 14:33, 41:7,
  45:26, 47:14, 73:22
COUNTRY DANCES (in titles)
  "Allmon Swiss," 2:52
  "Apollo," 3:25
  "Bricklayer," 17:45
  "Capt. Cook," 14:145
  "Columbia," 3:23 (with dance figures)
  "The cornplanter," 3:23
  "The Dutchess of Brumswick,"
    2:51
  "French," 18:13, 18:323, 84:38
  "The German," 14:37
  "The good girl," 3:7
  "Hob or nob," 47:14
  "Lucy's," 14:15
  "Major Strugeon," 5:68
  "Sally's favourite," 14:79
  "The seasons," 14:82
  "The white joke," 47:14
  "Widdow Dickens," 14:47
"The country farmer," m 5:76
"Country frolic," m 5:62
"The country weding," m 47:33
"The court of Vauxhall," m 5:145
"Courtier's think it no harm,"
  m 21:63
"Covent Garden," m 14:135
Covent Garden Theatre, 59, 64
Coventry, Countess of, 45:9

Coventry, Lady, 2:17, 17:8, 17:23,
   18:20, 18:226, 19:167, 20:12,
   32:54, 41:5, 47:24
"The cow in the haystack," m 2:31
Cowper, William, 4:81, 63
"A cradle hymn," mw 4:38
Cramer, Johann (John) Baptist,
   10:[1]
"Crazy Jane," m 21:62; mw 4:104,
   55:31
"Creamers sonata," m 18:103
"The cream pot," m 18:17
"The creelo," m 1:116
"The cricket," mw 4:81
The critic, "Air," m 5:93, 52:19
"The critick," m 14:16
"Crosby's," m 5:57
Crotch, William, 63
Crouch, Mrs. Anna Maria,
   50:24, 79:11
"A cruel fate hangs threatening,"
   mw 34:167
"Cruelle non, jamais," m 55:19
"Cruskine lamb," m 2:41
"The cuckoo," mw 15:1*v*, 47:37,
   50:66, 76:i
"The cuckoo's nest," m 5:71,
   13:76, 14:88, 47:5
"Cullodon fight," m 13:85
"Cumberland house," m 14:64
Cunningham, William, 20
"Cupid god of soft persuasion,"
   m 45:17, 45:18*v*
"Cupid's march," m 5:3, 43:9
"Cupid's recruiting seargent,"
   m 5:122, 13:50, 17:23, 21:75
Curtis Collections, 67
Curtiss, John F., 1
Custis, Eleanor Parke. *See* Lewis,
   Eleanor Parke Custis
Custis, George Washington Parke, 10
Cuzzoni, Sig[ra], 37:32
"Cymen and Iphigenia," mw 9:112
Cymon, "March, m 5:74; "Quick
   march," m 82:23
"Cynthia," m 14:75, 41:28;
   mw 4:102
Cyrowetz (composer), 49:62

"Dall fresque," m 32:20
"La dalle marque," m 5:119

"Dalston," m 80:153
"Damaetus aria," m 5:58
"Dame francois," m 5:11
"La damoiselle," m 11:14, 18:134,
   19:24, 47:55
"Damon & Clora," mw 37:48, 41:125,
   85:42
"Damon & Phyllis," m 2:9, 14:157
"Damon to Delia," mw 4:59
DANCE FIGURES, 2:49, 3:23, 38, 58
"Dance in *Queen Mab*," m 11:31
"Dance in *Tekeli*," m 80:102
"Dance in *The honeymoon*," m 49:82
DANCE MUSIC , 3, 5, 14, 37, 39, 52,
   59, 84. *See also* Entries under
   specific dance forms:
   ALLEMANDES,   COTILLIONS, COUNTRY
   DANCES, FANCIES, FANDANGOS, GAV-
   OTTES, HORNPIPES, JIGS, MINUETS,
   RANTS, REELS, STRATHSPEYS, WALTZES
DANCE MUSIC (in titles)
   "After the peasants dance," 14:155
   "All around the maypole," 41:7
   "The Bath figure," 84:45
   "Black dance," 13:93, 58:33
   "The celebrated chaccone or
      Spanish dance," 55:12
   "Celebrated tragic dance of Medea
      and Jason," 56
   "City dance," 47:17
   "Contredance," 32:43
   "Devils dance," 13:105
   "An English dance," 58:50
   "Fairy dance," 82:18
   "Favorite polonese," 49:70
   "Fife hunt - A favourit," 14:63
   "The first assembly," 38
   "The forist dance," 14:132
   "A French dance," 14:82
   "French dances," 18:224
   "German dance," 14:76, 14:139
   "Grand dance in *The 40 thieves*,"
      80:130
   "Hay makers dance," 3:24, 37:1, 41:9
   "Hessian dance," 5:39
   "Indian dance," 81:39
   "La petit ballet," 41:21
   "The ladies dance," 13:23
   "The little devil dance," 3:31
   "The London assembly," 45:42
   "Macaronia dance," 13:63
   "Merry dance," 21:74

DRAMATIC MUSIC (in titles)
  (*continued*)
  The honeymoon, 49:82
  Inkle and Yarico, 41:93,
    74:75, 77:24
  Judas Maccabeus, 5:84, 9:182, 35
  Judith, 9:205
  The lady of the lake, 15:21v
  Letho, 9:168
  Lionel and Clarissa, 34:147-57
  La Locanda, 7:13
  Lock & key, 76:56
  Lodoiska, 49:84, 50:24, 55:129,
    55:177, 81:27
  Love in a village, 5:152,
    34:159-61, 56
  The maid of the mill, 84:59, 84:67
  Matteruma, 81:47
  Merope, 5:83
  Messiah, 4:112-18
  Midas, 3:18
  The mountaineers, 1:145, 3:13,
    14:169, 17:34, 79:1
  My grandmother, 50:1
  No song no supper, 35:6
  Orpheus and Euridice, 47:1
  Oscar & Malvina, 1:20, 13:108a,
    15:31r, 15:36r, 49:60
  Paul and Virginia, 15:10v, 49:70
  Perseus and Andromeda, 37:3
  The pirates, 55:74
  Pizarro, 1:74
  The poor soldier, 3:36, 50:59, 85:27
  Porus, 67:22
  The purse, or Benevolent Tar,
    53:20(partially reduced
    score), 73:3
  The Quaker, 3:21
  Queen Mab, 5:44, 11:31, 37:2
  Robin Hood, 48
  Rosina, 1:22, 3:19-21, 3:32,
    27:27, 46:34, 50:26, 50:53[?],
    77:32, 79, 79:18-36 (reduced
    score), 83:14
  The royal shepherd, 59
  Samson, 9:188-90, 9:192, 47:17
  Saul, 5:78
  Scipio, 1:134, 57:1, 80:144
  Semaramis, 1:59
  Semele, 8:2, 9:195
  The Spanish barber, 5:97

DRAMATIC MUSIC (in titles)
  (*continued*)
  The spoiled child, 14:166,
    76:78, 77:29, 79:14-16
  The surrender of Calais,
    3:18, 73:27
  The sylvan, 56
  Tekeli, 80:102
  Theodora, 35
  Thomas and Sally, 34:23-55,
    47:13
  Two misers, 34:57-107
  The waterman, 34:163-66
  The whim of the moment, 46:41
  The woodman, 82:10
"The dream," mw 50:50
"The dressing room," m 47:35
"Dribs of brandy," m 14:12
"Drink to me only," m 1:11, 3:38,
  5:140, 14:34, 46:67, 80:157
"Drink to me only with thine eyes,"
  mw 77:1
"Drop a tear," m 14:162
"Drops of brandy," m 5:64, 43:3
"The drum," m 45:46
"The drummer's call," m 2:9,
  13:39, 43:7
"Drummond castle," m 14:9
"The drums call," m 11:20, 37:25
"The drums resound," mw 73:67
"Druncan house," m 13:95
"Drunk at night & dry in the
  morning," m 14:44
Dublin (Ireland), 14:5, 18:309,
  73:37
"Dublin tune," m 18:309
"Dubourg's minuet," m 18:422
"The dueler," m 14:67
"The duenna," m 14:69, 14:Kr
The duenna, "What bard, O time,
  discover," w 76
"Duet," m 1:6-18, 1:23, 1:160,
  49:2-5, 49:8-11, 49:12, 49:14,
  49:16, 49:18, 49:20, 49:22,
  49:24-39, 49:40-49, 49:50-53,
  49:56, 49:60, 49:66, 49:68,
  49:70-73, 49:74-77, 49:86-91
"Duet by Pleyel," m 1:34-35
"Duet for two harpsichords," m 8:37

DUETS, INSTRUMENTAL. *See* BASSOON
AND CLARINET MUSIC; CLARINET
MUSIC, 2 CLARINETS; FIFE
MUSIC, 2 FIFES; FLUTE AND
VIOLIN MUSIC; FLUTE MUSIC, 2
FLUTES; GUITAR MUSIC, 2 GUITARS;
HARPSICHORD MUSIC, 2 HARPSI-
CHORDS; KEYBOARD MUSIC, 2
KEYBOARDS; VIOLIN MUSIC,
2 VIOLINS

DUETS, INSTRUMENTAL (UNSPEC-
IFIED), 1, 3 (primo only),
4:82, 5:66, 5:86, 5:88-91,
6:60, 13:87, 13:94, 13:97-98,
14:139 (primo only), 14:162,
14:174 (primo only), 20:1,
20:3, 21:60, 37:41, 37:43,
37:51, 39, 80, 82:25

DUETS, VOCAL, 13:64, 21:57, 25,
37:48, 37:53, 41:125, 74:74,
77-78, 82:40; WITH KEYBOARD,
4:6, 4:17, 4:34, 4:41, 4:44,
4:55, 4:59, 4:84, 4:112, 7,
9, 15:10*v*, 15:28*v*, 15:40*v*, 16,
21:49, 22:8, 32:12, 32:15, 34,
53:50, 55:14, 55:97, 55:135,
67:18, 73, 75:12, 83:9, 83:42,
83:65-69

"Duettino," m 1:31, 1:84, 1:94,
1:152

"Duettino for two violins,"
m 1:162

"Duetto," m 1:86, 1:100, 1:102,
1:128, 1:132, 1:133, 1:146,
14:174, 49:60; mw 9:28, 9:91
9:109, 73:1, 83:67

"Duetto al Signr. Palma," m 9:43;
mw 9:25

"Duetto by Curtiss," m 1:98

"Duetto by Jean Baptisti Martini,"
m 1:38

"Duetto by Manienelli," m 1:140

"Duetto by Phillidore," m 1:87

"Duetto by Swindle," m 1:92, 1:144

"Duetto by Wuderhy," m 1:142

"Duetto tutto da voi dipende,"
mw 7:13

"Duke Hulisetons march," m 13:19

"Duke of Conflans cotillion," m 5:58

"Duke of Glosters march," m 47:72

"Duke of Gloster's new march,"
m 13:110, 18:380

"Duke of Gordon's birthday,"
m 14:71, 14:G*r*

"Duke of Holstein's march," m 1:63,
27:18, 48:23, 52:18

"Duke of Portland's waltz,"
m 48:38

"Duke of York's cotillion," m 48:36

"Duke of Yorks march," m 1:52, 1:72,
3:29, 4:122, 13:110, 14:115,
17:47, 18:330, 47:48, 52:63,
55:22, 58:24

"Duke of York's troop," m 47:50

"The duke's march," m 2:15, 5:53,
13:13, 37:25

"Dull care," m 15:1*r*

"Duncan Gray," mw 55:176

Dundee (Scotland), 14:44

"Dunfries house," 14:14

"Dunkeld house," m 14:33, 15:34*r*

"Duo," m 1:88, 1:150

Dupline, Lord, 14:18

Durang, John, 14:72, 14:B*r*, 73:82

"Durang's hornpipe," m 14:72,
14:B*r*, 73:82

"Durham march," m 27:17

Durham, [N. H.?], 26

"Dursd for sport," m 14:33

"The dusky night," m 5:148, 14:30,
41:11, 47:22, 52:59

"The dusky night rides down the
sky," mw 18:300

"The dust cart," mw 9:69

"The dusty miller," m 11:2

"The dutchess," m 14:19

"The Dutchess of Athol's strathpey,"
m 14:42

"The Dutchess of Brumswick country
dance," m 2:51

"Dutchess of York's fancy," m 14:64

"Dutchess slipper," m 48:43

"A Dutch realvry," m 84:47

"A Dutch Turks march," m 84:46

"Duval's hornpipe," m 14:43

"The dying Christian to his soul,"
mw 75:6, 83:5

"The dying Indian," m 81:39

"The dying lamb," mw 55 (sheet
pinned in)

The dying swan," m 80:18; mw 57:2
(textual incipit only)

"Faithful shepperdess," m 14:Lr
"Faithless Emma," mw 41:47
"The fall of Paris," m 15:2v
FANCIES (in titles)
  "Barnets," 5:59
  "Byrnes'," 73:80
  "Captain McKay's," 14:6
  "Capt. MacKintosh's," 3:3
  "Carroll's," 14:31
  "Dutches of York's," 14:64
  "The fancy," 14:43
  "Fany's," 14:77
  "Jenny's," 14:73
  "Johnson's," 14:73
  "Lady Montague's," 14:37
  "Lady Townsend's," 14:79
  "Lady Worsley's," 14:137
  "Lewis's," 19:146
  "McKays," 14:90
  "Major Porter's," 14:78
  "Miss Heard's," 14:131
  "Miss Jackson's," 14:127
  "Miss Peke's," 14:132
  "Miss Poots," 81:28
  "Miss Reilly's," 14:126
  "Miss Robinson's," 14:8
  "Mr. Evans," 14:42
  "Wilke's," 14:79
"The fancy," m 14:43
"Fandango," m 3:24
FANDANGOS (in titles)
  "The new," 14:20, 14:136
"Fanny's toy," m 14:57
"Fany's fancy," m 14:77
"Farewell, farewell, a sad long
  farewell," mw 6:63
"Farewell to country friends," m 5:35
"Farewell to Elizabeth Town," m 2:15
"Farewell to Locharber," mw 9:136
"Farewell to the green fields,"
  m 2:30, 49:1
"Farewell to wives and sweet-
  hearts," m 37:3
"Farewell ye green fields,"
  m 17:24, 45:56, 46:63, 80:117
The farmer, "Ere around the hugh
  oak, mw 35:20; "The madrigal,"
  m 3:12, "My Daddy oh was very
  good," m 3:11
"The farrago," m 1:40
"Father knows his own house,"
  m 43:9
"Favorite, &c.," m 17:27

"The favorite additional rondo in
  Castle of Andalusia," mw 55:23
"A favorite air," m 14:151,
  27:27, 49:22
"A favorite air by Mr. Arne,"
  m 47:76
"Favorite air by Stamitz,"
  m 1:28. *See also* "Stamitz' air"
"A favorite allemande," m 14:173,
  49:62
"A favorite catch," mw 30:10
"A favorite French march," m 17:12
"A favorite Irish air," m 45:66
"A favorite jig," m 11:30, 47:40
"Favorite la chasse by J. C.
  Moller," m 76:1
"A favorite lesson," m 18:371-72,
  19:133
"A favorite lesson for the piano-
  forte," m 18:280
"A favorite march," m 14:114,
  14:Cv, 58:39
"A favorite march in 'The demo-
  lition of the Bastile,'" m 80:93
"A favorite minuet," m 18:108,
  18:392
"The favorite mock cuckow solo,"
  m 14:88
"The favorite new federal song,"
  mw 55:21, 79:17
"The favorite overture to ...'Medee
  and Jason,'" m 56
"Favorite polonese," m 49:70
"A favorite Scotch song," m 17:45
"The favorite seraneding,"
  m 18:137
"A favorite sonata by Nicholai,"
  m 83:46
"A favorite song in *Artaxerxes*,"
  mw 84:30
"A favt song in *Inkle & Yarico*,"
  mw 77:24
"A favorite song...in...*Lodoiska*,"
  mw 50:24
"Favorite song in *The spoil'd child*,"
  mw 77:29
"The favorite song out of *Castle
  Andalusia*," mw 85:14
"A favorite Venetian ballad,"
  m 14:172
"A favorite waltz," m 15:15v

FREEMASON MUSIC (in titles)
(*continued*)
"March for the Appollo Lodge,"
14:97
"The Mason's anthem," 67:8
"Mason's farewell," 52:31
"To all who Masonry despise,"
67:5
"Freemasons farewell," m 6:45
"Freemasons march," m 6:27, 11:6,
11:14, 13:4, 14:32, 21:43,
27:16, 37:23, 43:19, 45:74
"A French air," m 14:74, 41:25,
49:48, 49:54, 80:104,
80:159, 83:14(2)
"French allemand," m 5:8
"French Catherine," m 2:37
"A French cotillion," m 15:17*v*
"French country dance," m 18:13,
18:323, 84:38
"A French dance," m 14:82, 18:224
"The French detilyan quick," m 2:42
"The French grenadiers," m 37:25
"The French grenadiers march,"
m 14:112, 43:13
"French grenadiers salute," m 43:13
"French guard's march," m 81:55
"A French horn tune," m 84:39
"French march," m 11:29, 19:151
"The French marriens march,"
m 84:42
"French minuet," m 20:11, 41:3
"French National Guards march,"
m 1:27
"French quick march," m 13:102
"French presto," m 19:121b
"French solo allegro," m 18:227
"A French song," m 14:175
FRENCH SONGS. *See* SONGS IN FRENCH
"The French troop," m 2:40, 13:26
"Fresh & strong," m 3:9, 6:62,
13:94, 80:112; mw 15:5*r*,
41:93 (2 textual lines only)
"Fresh and strong the breeze is
blowing," mw 17:42, 76:44,
80:30, 83:78
"The fresh water sailor," m 13:79
"The friar & nun," m 37:45
"Friend & pitcher," m 11:11;
mw 4:132. *See also* "My friend
and pitcher"

"The friendly society," m 14:153
"Friendship," m 13:12, 13:93,
15:27*r*, 37:27, 37:29, 80:141
"Friendship to the willing mind,"
mw 4:32
"The frisky," m 14:29, 14:154,
47:60
"Frog & mouse," m 14:68, 52:23
"From sweet bewitching tricks
of love," mw 9:139
"From the east banks the morn,"
m 47:51
"From the east breaks the morn,"
m 5:129
"From the man whom I love," m 5:13
"From thee Eliza I must go," mw 76:77
"From whence, Louisa, comes the
fire," mw 46:58
"The frozen streets in moonshine
glitter," mw 83:34
Fuld, James J., 41-44
"Funeral dirge," mw 6:63
"Funeral song," mw 15:21*v*

"Gaily the troubadour touched his
guitar," mw 15:43*v*
"The galland soldier," m 80:134
"Gallant sailor," m 5:73
"The galley slave," m 11:7, 14:B*r*,
15:16*v*, 41:95, 52:39;
mw 4:106, 53:44
"The galley slave's complaint,"
m 47:21
"Galloping dreary dun," m 5:47
"Galloway Tom," m 5:13
Gambier, Captain, 84:5
"Gaminianis minuet," m 18:414
GAMUT: FLUTE, 47:ii; KEYBOARD,
46:62; VIOLIN, 14
"Gang we yon," m 14:12
"Ganz war ich," m 85:8
Gardiner, Mrs., 84:4
"The garland," mw 9:111
"Garners hornpipe," m 14:124
Garrick, David, 1, 72, 85:39
"Garrick rant," m 84:64
"The garter," m 47:75
Garth, John, 18:338
"Gates are barr'd a vain resis-
tance," mw 35:2
"The gathering," m 13:106

"The Gesuit," m 45:62
Giardini, Felice de, 9:191, 85:39
"Giddy giddy gout your shirt hangs out," mw 7:5
"Giga," m 8:24, 11:38, 18:397
"Giga by Corelli," m 18:419
"Giga by Leonard," m 18:417
"Giga by Mr. Wolff," m 18:400
"Giga by Sig'r Dubourg," m 18:423
"Gigue," m 55:93, 58:15, 60:4, 76:16, 80:7. See also "Jig;" "Jigg"
"Gigue par Correlli," m 85:24
"Gilderoy," m 13:65, 14:114, 17:31, 85:30
Giles, Debby, 21
Gillingham, George, 72
"Gin loving worth cou'd win my heart," mw 74:68
"Ginney's got hair on it," m 47:inside front cover
Giordani, Giuseppe or Tommaso, 35:4, 41:27, 55:23, 59
"Giordani's minuet," m 41:27
"A gipsy ballad," mw 4:91
"The girl I left behind me," m 13:18, 14:55
"Girls take care of your towrowron," m 47:inside front cover
"Give me the sweet delights of love," mw 30:17
"Give round the word," m 5:142, 14:7, 46:12
Glasgow (Scotland), 67
"Glee by Mr. Purcell," mw 30:35
GLEES, 30, 34:167, 80:118
"The glideing streams," m 78:35
"Glorious craft which fires the mind," mw 67:4
"The glorious 12th of April," m 14:137
Gloucester, Duke of, 13:110, 18:380, 47:72
"The Gloucestershire march," m 5:72
Gluck, Christoph Willibald, Ritter von, 56
"Go & come," m 14:47
"Go false Damon go," mw 37:48 85:42
"Go happy insect flit thy way," mw 4:14

"Go patter to lubber and swab," mw 46:41
"Go rose, my Chloe's bosom grace," mw 9:64
"Go to her hands," mw 50:54
"Go to the devil and shake yourself," m 13:59, 13:96, 14:17 52:24
"The god of love," m 3:15, 4:103, 4:108
The god of love, "March," m 11:5, 14:98, 27:14, 49:4, 58:14
"God save America," m 48:13; mw 24:59
"God save America free from despotic sway," w 74:15
"God save Columbia," m 49:1
"God save great George the Third," m 17:32
"God save great Washington," m 17:32
"God save the king," m 1:1, 5:120, 6:31, 18:40, 20:6, 45:10, 45:37, 47:1, 74:16, 80:36, 82:1
"The golden days," m 3:38
Goldsmith, Oliver, 73:37
"The good girl," m 3:7
"Good morrow to your night cap," m 5:131, 11:16, 32:18, 73:111
Goostre, Mr., 47:54
Gordan, Captain, 2:12
Gordon, Duke of, 14:71, 14:Gr
Gore, Lord, 14:104
"Gore's march," m 48:13
"Gossop, for peace sake half it," m 14:48
Govane, Archduke, 67
"Gov. Jays march," m 1:71, 52:53. See also "Jay's march"
"Governor Strong's march," m 49:64, 81:69
"The graceful move," mw 41:133
"Graceful mov'd," m 5:17
"The graces," m 14:137, 14:143, 46:3
"Gramachree," m 2:35, 32:23, 41:34
"Gramachree Molly," m 45:30, 45:75; mw 21:66
"Gramachree my Molly," m 17:5
Granby, Marquis of, 2:18, 5:121, 14:116, 27:16, 45:17, 45:63, 47:6
"Grand dance in The 40 thieves," m 80:47, 80:130

Hall, Mrs. Katy, 11:33
Hamilton, Charles, 41
"Hamiltons house," m 47:82
"Hancock," mw 80:71
Handel, George Frederic, 1:2, 1:70,
    1:78, 1:82, 1:134, 4:41, 4:82-83,
    4:112, 4:127, 5:31, 5:80, 8:2,
    9:74-87, 9:148, 9:182, [9:188-90,
    9:192-97], 14:102, 14:158,
    17:16, 18:324, 18:346, 18:368,
    18:418, 19:168, 35:66-84, 35:32,
    37:17, 43:7, 47:31, 49:58, 52:25,
    80:18, 80:112, 81:37, 81:78-79,
    84:14
"Handel's clarinet," m 1:2, 4:83,
    5:31, 19:168
"Handel's clarinet duet," m 17:16
"Handel's clarionett," m 49:58,
    81:37, 81:79
"Handel's march," m 43:7
"Handel's trumpet," m 14:102
"Handel's waterpiece," m 1:78,
    4:82, 5:80, 18:346, 37:17,
    47:31, 81:78
"Hand's minuet," m 47:58
"The handsome daughter," m 14:90
"Handsome Pattie," m 5:70
"Hang me if I marry," m 47:3
"Hanover tune," m 18:306
"The happy Bacchanalian," m 5:143
"Happy clown," m 5:2
"Happy flock of Christ thy
    Saviour," mw 83:67
"Happy, happy, happy pair,"
    mw 9:86
"Happy hours," m 5:148
"The happy marriage," m 85:32
"The happy pair," m 5:57
"The happy soldier," m 14:24
"The happy wedding," m 5:45
"Harcasom's duett," m 14:139
"Hare in the corn," m 5:62, 37:12
Harington (Harrington), Henry,
    30:3, 30:5, 30:15, 30:17,
    30:19, 85:40
"Harisons compound march," m 6:34
"Hark-away," mw 41:36 (textual 1st
    line only)
"Hark away is the word," m 46:2
"Hark hark hark her sweet voice
    all plaintive sounds," mw 84:1

"Hark hark the joy inspiring horn,"
    m 47:74
"Hark 'tis I your own true lover,"
    mw 84:67
"Hark the goddess Diana," mw
    15:40*v*, 55:97
"Hark the herald angels sing,"
    mw 53:42
"Hark! the huntsman's begun,"
    mw 5:87, 47:51
"Hark this loud drum," mw 84:86
"Hark while our ship is springing,"
    mw 21:48
Harlequin, "The dressing room,"
    m 47:35
Harlequin's invasion, "Come cheer up
    my lads," mw 84:12; "Overture,"
    m 72; "Song," m 57:33
Harlequin sorcerer, "Ye chearfull
    virgins have ye seen," mw 84:15
"Harliqueau's geneology drage," m 2:33
Harmonia sacra, 4:38-40
"Harmonie concert," m 1:82
HARPSICHORD: INSTRUCTIONS FOR
    TUNING, 55
HARPSICHORD MUSIC, 8, 18:372,
    19; 2 HARPSICHORDS, 8:37
Harrington, Henry. *See* Harington
    (Harrington), Henry
"The Harriot," m 52:21
Harris Collection, 73-75
Hart, D., Colonel, 2:38
"Hartland," m 43:19
"Hartley," mw 80:41
"Harvest home," m 5:120
Harwood, J. E., 54:16-21
Hasse, Johann Adolph, 47:35,
    56:28
"Haste to the wedding," m 15:18*r*,
    18:374. *See also* "Come haste to
    the wedding"
"Haste ye soft gales," mw 30:10
"Haunted lover," m 13:107
The haunted tower, "Celebrated air,"
    m 1:7; "French air [?]," m
    80:104; "My native land,"
    mw 35:10
"The hautboy," m 13:65
"Have mercy Lord on me," mw 80:46
Hawkins, Micah, 47
"The hay in the hay stack," m 37:15
"The hayden," m 3:15

"The highland man kiss'd his
mother," m 14:54
"The highland march," m 5:67,
15:31*r*, 15:36*r*, 85:28
"Highland queen," m 5:89,
85:28; mw 4:89, 41:105
"Highland reel," m 18:23, 18:222,
19:2, 73:88
"The highland wedding," m 13:80
"Highland's march," m 45:71
Hilligsberg, Madam, 14:58
"Himno patiotica guerro," 55
"Hither ye faithful haste with
songs of triumph," mw 15:3*v*
"Hob nob," m 15:22*v*. *See also*
"New hob nob"
"Hob or nob," m 2:34, 5:10, 13:3,
47:14, 48:32, 52:16
"Hobbinol," m 37:47
"Hobson's choice," m 14:52
Hodgkinson, Mrs., 50:48
"Hollis," m 80:153
"The hollow drum," m 13:16, 21:74,
52:23; mw 53:46
Holstein, Duke of, 1:63, 27:18,
48:23, 52:18, 81:71
"Holstine's march," m 81:71
"Holts minuet," m 18:421
"Holy and fairly," m 47:73
Holyoke, Samuel, 13:82
"Homeward bound," mw 73:63
"The honble Miss Rolles reel,"
m 14:62
"The honey moon," m 14:82; mw 77:37
The honeymoon, "Dance," m 49:82
"Hook & crook," mw 4:72
Hook, James, 1:41, 1:90, 10:188,
10:194, 17:40, 18:293, 18:383,
35:24, 50:18, 50:45, 53:31-41,
73:35, 75:14-17, 81:32,
85:38, 85:40
Hooke, George Philip, 30
"Hooke's march," m 14:117
"Hope," mw 41:129
Hope, Lady Harriett, 2:14 [lacking],
14:37
"Hope thou nurse," m 5:103,
47:23, 82:3
"Hope! Thou nurse of young desire,"
mw 50:32
Hopkins, Robert E., 12

Hopkinson, Francis, 9, 9:63, 9:111,
9:163, 9:169, 9:179-80, 24,
33, 55
Hopkinson, Joseph, 79:17
Horn, Colonel, 14:103
"A hornpipe," m 2:26, 2:34, 11:32,
13:102-4, 80:44, 84:28
"Hornpipe gervot in Otho," m 13:82
HORNPIPES (in titles)
"Astleys," 80:7, 80:80
"Bakers," 11:37
"Black Marys," 11:8
"Bob's," 14:49
"Chalk's," 45:3
"Clarke's," 47:17
"College," 5:12, 11:10, 13:104,
15:18*r*, 18:395, 37:18, 47:2,
60:5
"Durang's," 14:72, 14:8*r*, 73:82
"Duval's," 14:43
"Fisher's," 3:19, 13:37, 14:57,
15:3*v*, 18:421, 45:50,
52:25, 58:40
"Frances's," 37:15
"Garners," 14:124
"Gavot in Otho," 13:82
"Master Linley's," 45:6
"The milk maids," 37:22
"The new century," 48:41
"Huss hills," 14:64
"Mann's," 13:98
"Miss Blake's," 2:31
"Miss Hunter's," 14:55
"Miss West's," 14:133
"Mrs. Baker's," 2:25, 5:27
"Mrs. Vernon's," 45:7, 47:10
"Nancy Dawson's," 5:49
"O'Derige's," 14:87
"Richer's," 14:58
"Rickard's," 14:54
"Ricketts," 3:19
"Robinson's," 14:57
"Rolling," 13:28, 37:16
"Rooling," 13:18
"Rudleam," 13:103
"The sailor's," 2:37
"Saunder's second," 14:58
"The Staden Isleland," 18:14
"Stepneys," 13:37
"Tom Tollese's," 14:84
"Woods," 13:102
"The Werth," 13:103

"Lucky kitchen," m 5:75
"Lucy Campbell afternoon," m 14:71
"Lucy's birth right," m 14:123
"Lucy's country dance," m 14:15
"Lucy's delight," m 14:78, 47:34
"Lullaby," m 14:167; mw 76:74
"Lullees croacker," m 13:14
Lully, Jean Baptiste de, 18:412,
    84:18
"Lully's minuet," m 18:412
"La lumiere," m 3:36, 14:179
LUTE, 1 (illustration)
"Lyra," m 14:51

"Ma belle coquette," mw 73:5
"Ma chère amie," m 4:108
"Ma chère amie, my charming fair,"
    mw 17:39, 32:16
"Macaronia dance," m 13:63
McDonald, Lord, 14:37, 14:104,
    48:8, 79:9
"McDonald's favourite," m 14:41
"McDonald's rant," m 14:53
McDowell, David, 14:62
McKay, Captain, 14:6
"McKays fancy," m 14:90
McKinie, William, 67
MacKintosh, Captain, 3:3, 4:124,
    14:43
"McPherson's farewell," m 17:45
"Madam Hilligsberg's reel,"
    m 14:58
"Madam Plaud's allemand," m 1:1
"The madrigal," m 3:12, 14:30,
    81:11
"Madrigal imitated from the Spanish
    by Mr. Garrick," 85:39
"The magazine," m 14:86
"Maggie Lawder," m 5:100, 12:19,
    17:22, 19:48, 24, 37:10,
    45:45, 82:4
"Le mai turbo il tuo riposo," mw 9:4
"Maid in the pump room," m 13:5,
    21:73
"The maid of Martindale," mw 50:45
"Maid of the mill," m 11:14, 47:47
The maid of the mill, "Free from
    sorrow, free from grief," mw
    84:59, 84:65; "Hark, 'tis I
    your own true lover," mw 84:67

"Maid of the oak," m 17:15, 47:17
"The maid to my mind,"
    m 85:40
"Maidens gallop," m 5:59
"Majestic rose the god of day,"
    mw 75:18
"Major André's complaint," mw 53:19.
    See also "André's complaint;"
    "A song of Major Andrea"
"Major minor," m 14:163, 21:24, 80:54
"Majr Porter's fancy by Carroll,"
    m 14:78
"Major Strugeon," m 5:68
"Majors maggot," m 11:35
"Malbrook," m 1:82, 5:137, 6:10,
    18:9, 32:21, 47:47, 48:17,
    76:7, 82:17
Man (composer). *See* Mann, Elias
"The man in the moon," m 5:73,
    18:222, 19:2
"Mananio," m 13:33
Manienelli (composer), 1:140
Mann, Elias, 4:20
"Mann's hornpipe," m 13:98
"Marble hall," m 37:1
"Marbrough duetto," m 17:26
"March," m 1:120, 37:20(2), 37:36,
    46:6, 46:22, 46:32, 49:14,
    49:56, 58:5, 58:13, 58:20,
    58:23, 58:39, 81:57, 81:65
"March à la militaire," m 49:72
"March at coronation," m 1:135
"March battle piece," m 15:36r
"March by Handel in *The constela-
    teon*," m 1:70
"March by Heydn," m 1:155
"March...by Phi. Roth," m 46:38
"March by Wilson," m 80:5, 80:143
"March debose," m 14:104, 14:108
"March for Bonaparte's Imperial
    Guard," m 51:50v
"March...for Col. Lee's legion of
    horses," mw 46:38
"March for many instruments,"
    mw 84:86
"March for the Appollo Lodge,"
    m 14:97
"March Ieseware," m 58:41
"March in *Abaellino*," m 49:62
"March in *Abelinio*," m 82:24
"March in 'A midnight serenade,'"
    m 1:64

"Oh Lord that art my righteous judge," mw 9:175
"O Lord thou art my God," m 82:40
"O love what the deauce do you want," m 82:12
"Oh my bonny Bet," m 3:3
"O my little saylor boy," m 14:93
"O Nanny whilt thou gang with me," m 41:32; w 41:78
"Oh nightingale best poet of the grove," mw 4:88
"Oh Peace thou fairest child of heav'n," mw 9:128
"O sanctissima purissima dulcis Virgo Maria," mw 15:34r
"Oh Sandy why leav'st thou thy Nelly to mourn," mw 84:84
"Oh say bonny lass," mw 74:75
"O say can you see," w 41:82
"Oh say have you seen my Mary seen the Caledonian maid," mw 10:197, 73:73, 79:3
"Oh say not woman's love is bought," mw 15:42r
"O say simple maid," mw 41:93, 74:75, 77:3, 77:24
"O say what is that thing call'd light," mw 76:15
"Oh sleep, oh sleep why dost thou leave me," mw 9:195
"Oh Sylvia while you drive your carts," mw 9:69
"Oh! tell me softly breathing gale," mw 35:58
"Oh that I had wings like a dove," mw 30:13
"Oh! think on my fate," mw 4:106, 56:44
"Oh whistle and I will come to you my lad," mw 15:7r
"Oh! why should I weep," mw 54:2
"Oh wouldst thou know," mw 9:52
"Oh young Lochinvar is come," mw 15:23r
"The oak," m 6:48
"The oake stick," m 47:75
O Blaney, Murdoch, 5:55, 14:15
O'Bosvil, Captain, 14:63
O'Bryan, Mr., 84:6
Occasional Oratorio, "March," m 13:109, 47:27

"Ode on science," mw 23:38
"An ode on spring," mw 73:29
"Ode on the death of Dr. Franklin," mw 53:16
"Ode, sung at the arrival of the President of the United States," w 74:16
"Ode to Delia," mw 50:54
"O'Derige's hornpipe," m 14:87
O'er. *See* Over
"Of all sensation pity brings," mw 40:3
"Of all the swains both near nad far," mw 53:56
"Of Bray the vicar," mw 4:63
"The off fool Tom Rower," m 37:24
"Off she goes," m 11:40
"Officers dinner drum," m 13:106
"The oft flowing Avon," m 14:176
O Guire, Shilley, 5:38
Oh. *See* O
O'Hara, General, 5:25
Ohio River, 14:132, 47:20
"L'oiseau royal," m 45:11
"Old Buffs quick step," m 11:13
"Old Chaucer once, to this re echoing grove," mw 9:120
"Old continental march," m 11:12
"Old England my toast," m 47:56
"Old Father John," m 37:19
"Old Fowler," m 37:31, 82:11; mw 83:75
"Old hundred," m 80:153
"The old maid," m 13:66, 13:70 (title only)
"The old man," m 13:16, 37:18
"Old Robin Gray," m 81:14. *See also* "Auld Robin Gray"
Old Sturbridge Village, 15, 21-26
"Old wife beyond the fire," m 14:46
"The old woman," m 13:8, 14:20
"Old woman tost in a blanket," m 3:27
"The old woman's oratory," m 14:75, 37:21
O'Meara, Eva J., 1
"Omsted's duett," m 14:162
"On cherub's wings Jehovah comes," mw 80:49
"On my heart the wounds forever be inscrib'd," mw 83:72-74

"On on my dear brethren," m 67:12
"On pleasures smooth wings,"
    m 45:20
"On Primrose Hill there lived a
    lass," mw 22:20
"On Richmond Hill there lives a
    lass," mw 4:94, 10:190, 53:4
"On spring," mw 41:122
"On the green sedgy banks of the
    sweet winding Tay," mw 74:70
"On the way to Boston," m 43:15
"On the way to the field," m 43:5
"One day I heard Mary say,"
    mw 10:182
"One fond kiss before we part,"
    mw 58:37
"The one hundred psalm," m 18:308,
    57:14. *See also* "Psalm 100"
"136th psalm tune," m 80:151
"Open the door to thee," m 14:9
"The opera reel," m 14:125
OPERAS, 3:32, 9:195; (in titles)
    see DRAMATIC MUSIC (in titles)
"The orange grove," m 14:52
"The orange tree," m 14:45
ORATORIOS, 9:188-90, 9:192, 9:196;
    by Handel, 35; "Occasional,"
    47:27. *See also* DRAMATIC MUSIC
ORGAN MUSIC, 18:110-33, 18:379,
    18:402, 18:416, 18:418
"Organ piece," m 18:416
ORNAMENTATION, 1, 77:1
Orne, Colonel, 13:63, 27:28
"Orne's march," m 4:101
"The orphan's prayer,"
    mw 83:34
Orpheus and Euridice, "Comick
    tune," m 47:1
"Oscar and Malvina," m 13:108a
Oscar & Malvina, "The Caledonian
    hunt," m 15:36r; "Highland
    march," m 15:31r, 15:36r;
    "March battle piece," m 15:36r;
    "Overture," m 15:31r, 15:36r;
    "Quick march," m 1:20, 49:60
Oswego, N. Y., 14:32
Otho, "Hornpipe gervot," m 13:82
Otway, Lady, 14:176
"Our country," m 1:114
"Our glory renown'd on the ocean
    and shore," mw 84:82

"Our loves when ye shepherds shall
    view," mw 9:160
"Our pleasure," m 5:85, 14:24, 73:7
"O'er barren hills and flowr'y
    dales," mw 32:52, 53:25
"Over the heather among the moors,"
    m 14:134
"Over the hills and far away,"
    m 5:60, 11:32, 47:46
"Over the hills and vallies gone,"
    m 13:44
"Over the moor," m 13:43, 80:4
"Over the river to Charley," m 37:13
"Over the water to Charley," m 5:10,
    11:25, 45:13, 47:7, 81:31, 85:36
"Overture," m 18:50, 18:282,
    18:350-67, 71, 83:69
"Overture de Semele," m 8:2
"Overture Edelmann," m 56
"Overture in *Love in a village*,"
    m 56
"Overture of *Delasaina*," m 46:46
"Overture to *Harlequins invasion*,"
    m 72
"Overture to *Lodoiska*," m 55:129
"Overture to *Oscar and Malvina*,"
    m 15:31r, 15:36r
"Overture to *Rosina*," m 79:21
"Overture to *The deserter*,"
    m 14:171, 15:5v, 46:24, 53:29
"Overture to The sylvan," m 56
OVERTURES: 2 FLUTES, 46:24, 46:46;
    KEYBOARD, 15:10, 18:50, 18:282,
    18:350-67, 53:29, 55:129, 56,
    83:14, 83:25, 83:69; ORCHESTRA,
    8:67 (reduced score), 15:31r
    and 36r (reduced score), 79:21
    (reduced score); PIANO, 8:2,
    8:67; STRING QUARTET, 68-72;
    VIOLIN, 14:171; 2 VIOLINS,
    46:24, 46:46
"The owen," m 6:52, 81:29
"Oxford camp," m 14:73
"Oxford exile," m 1:45
"Oxford road to Pantheon," m 3:17
"Oxford to the Pantheon," m 17:14
"The oysterwifes rant," m 11:17

Pachelbel, Mr., 57:10
"Paddy Carey," m 15:27r

"Richmond grenadiers march,"
  m 14:147
"Rickard's hornpipe," m 14:54
"Ricketts hornpipe," m 3:19
"Ride a cock horse to Banbury]
  Cross," mw 7:6
"The rigg'd ship," m 14:7
"The rights of women," m 14:17,
  18:222, 19:2
"Rise Collumbia," m 80:88
"Rise Cynthia rise," m 49:68,
  58:58; mw 4:102, 53:33, 73:35
"Rise, rise, rise, heart breaking
  sighs," mw 9:172
"Ritorna al caro bene," mw 9:22
"The river," m 13:3
"Roanoke waltz," m 77:46
"The roast beef of old England,"
  m 2:21, 11:29
"Roast goose," m 37:21
"Robi down," m 11:37
"Robin Hood," m 14:160
Robin Hood, "Finale," 48 [lacking]
"Robinson's hornpipe," m 14:57
Robinson, Miss, 14:8
Rochester, N. Y., 53
Rockingham, Marquis of, 5:52
"Rodney for ever," m 14:137
Rogers, David, 2
"Roguara doo," m 14:21
"The rogues march," m 2:36, 6:50,
  13:23, 43:15, 80:113
Rolle, Johann Heinrich, 32:15
Rolle, Miss, 14:62
"The rolling hornpipe," m 13:28,
  37:16
"Romance," m 5:74; mw 55:126
"The romantics of the forest,"
  m 1:138
Romeo and Juliet, "A solemn dirge,"
  mw 9:172
"The romp," m 5:65
"Rondeau," m 46:20; mw 9:191
"Rondo," m 1:16, 1:125, 1:127,
  14:138, 15:8r, 15:12v, 18:107,
  18:139, 18:143, 18:147, 18:156,
  18:181, 18:221, 18:223, 18:386,
  18:425, 19:133, 19:135, 19:138,
  19:156, 19:158, 19:160, 19:162,
  19:164-65, 32:33, 32:42,
  46:4(2), 46:24, 49:24, 49:48,
  49:58, 58:30, 83:38, 83:53,

"Rondo" (*continued*)
  83:59, 85:5, 85:17(2)
"Rondo air Ecossais," m 55:18
"Rondo allegretto by Nicolai,"
  m 18:264
"Rondo allegro by Garth," m 18:338
"Rondo allegro by Nicolai," m 18:270
"Rondo by Hook," m 1:41, 18:382
"Rondo by Phi Roth," m 58:25
"Rondo Kozeluch," m 56
"Rondo of the grand overture of
  Martini," m 46:28
"Rooling hornpipe," m 13:18
"The rope dance," m 14:80
Rorther, Lord, 14:147
"Rosa," mw 75:18
"The rosary," m 41:41
"The rose," m 5:14, 41:17, 47:3,
  82:15; mw 4:50, 9:101, 77:9
"The rose and thorn," m 5:133
"The rose bud," m 14:76
"The rose had been wash'd,"
  mw 41:100, 63
"Rose in a castle," m 47:inside back cover
"The rose of Allandale," mw 15:45r
"The rose tree," m 3:13, 6:45,
  13:75, 15:16r, 46:64, 47:11,
  48:25, 52:43, 80:38, 81:60
"A rose tree full in bearing,"
  mw 18:292, 32:14
Rosencrantz (composer), 49:86-91
"The rosetta," m 14:8
Rosina, "Air," m 1:22, 27:27, 83:14;
  "The bird of the rose," m 46:34;
  "Finale," m 3:32; "Fisher's
  hornpipe," m 3:19;"Her mouth,
  which a smile," mw 79:35; "The
  morn returns in saffron drest,"
  m 3:20; mw 79:33; "Overture,"
  m 79:21; "Song," m 79:36 (incomplete); "Sweet transports
  gentle wishes go," mw 79:18;
  "Taste of pleasures, ye who
  may," mw 50:53; "When the rosy
  morn appearing," m 3:20; "When
  William at eve," m 3:21; mw 79:20;
  "Whilst with village maids I
  stray," mw 50:26, 79:32
"Rosina DeLit," m 14:43
"Roslin castle," m 1:48, 2:25, 6:47,
  11:12, 14:164, 15:17r, 17:13,
  18:28, 32:11, 37:27, 45:35,

Shattuck, Abel, 13
Shaw, Oliver, 80:95
"Shays," m 37:36
"Shay's march," m 14:54,
    21:74, 52:57
"She never thinks of me," mw 50:70
"The sheep had in clusters,"
    m 5:15. *See also* "Her sheep
    had in clusters"
"Sheep in thy clusters," m 14:67;
    mw 4:6
"Sheep sherer's dance," m 14:136
Sheldy (composer), 18:222
Shepherd, Levi, 17
Shepherd, Miss, 84:4
Shepherd, Thomas, 17
"The shepherd Adonis," mw 17:32
"A shepherd wander'd we are told,"
    mw 77:25
"The shepherdess," mw 74:74
"The shepherds complaint," m 80:20;
    mw 4:88
"Shepherds I have lost my love,"
    m 45:70; mw 15:4r, 41:130,
    76:66
"The shepherds plain life,"
    mw 9:131
"Sherburne," m 80:151
"She's compleat from top to
    tow," m 47:54
Shield, William, 10:175, 10:196,
    35:1, 35:16, 35:20, 59, 64,
    79, 83:75
"Shilinagigg," m 14:86
"Shilley O Guire," m 5:38
"Shilli Ocary," m 18:314
"Shingley's allemand," m 47:16
"Short troop," m 81:75
Shuster (composer), 53:8
"The Sicilian hymn," mw 15:34r
"Sicilian mariner's hymn," m 49:62,
    80:117
"The Sicilian peasant," m 14:9,
    17:28, 47:74
Sidness, Sir Charles, 1:29
"Signior La Clair's minuet,"
    m 14:171
"Silvander," m 4:11
"The silver moon," mw 53:36,
    76:68; w 4:145v
"Silver street," m 80:57

"Simfonia," m 46:36. *See also*
    "Symphonia"
"Simsons whim," m 47:80
"Since Kathlean has proved so untrue,"
    m 3:36
"Since love is the plan," m 5:112,
    73:30
"Since then I'm doom'd," mw 76:78,
    79:14
"Sinclears farewell," m 81:24
"Sing we praise to the Lord,"
    mw 9:157
SINGING, INSTRUCTIONS FOR, 21:4,
    25, 42
"Singling of Pools troop,"
    m 13:108
"Sir Charles Sidness minuett,"
    m 1:29
"Sr. George Saville's march,"
    m 84:51
"Sir Sidney Smith's minuett," m 1:5
"Sir you are a comical fellow,"
    m 47:61
"Sister! Sister!" mw 30:1
"The sisters," mw 75:14
"The six of diamonds," m 2:53
"The 16th Regt. march," m 14:99
"The 68th Regt. march," m 14:101
"The skaiting duetto," m 46:12
"The sky lark," m 18:244
"A slave to the fair," m 47:39
"Sleep on, sleep on my Kathleen
    dear," mw 85:26
"The sleeping daughter," mw 4:31
"Slingsby's allamande," m 14:29,
    32:20
"Slow march," m 13:100, 48:35,
    49:78(2)
"Smile America," m 5:9
"A smile from the girl of my heart,"
    m 82:10
"The smiling morn the breathing
    spring," mw 41:127; w 41:134
"Smiling Polly," m 47:75
Smith (composer), 43:27
Smith, Mrs., 3:39
Smith, Sir Sidney, 1:5
Smith, [William?], 80:57
"The snakey hills," m 14:123
"Snatch fleeting pleasures,"
    mw 76:82

"So merrily dance the Quakers,"
  m 5:66
"So sweet was young Damon," mw 9:107
Soam, Miss, 18:109
"The social pow'rs," m 41:12,
  47:79. *See also* "Come mow all
  ye social powers;" "Ye social
  powr's"
"Soft be the gently breathing
  notes," m 21:49; w 21:44
"Soft is the zephirs," m 79:8
"Soft murmurs," mw 77:1
"Soft zephr on thy bonny wing,"
  mw 54:6
"The soldier," m 14:159; mw 4:3
"Soldier, soldier," mw 30:9
"A soldier I am for a lady,"
  m 5:86; mw 73:31
"A soldier is the lad for me,"
  m 5:141, 14:68, 47:52
"The soldier lassie," m 47:57
"The soldier's adieu," m 14:161,
  81:40
"The soldiers delight," m 37:19
"Soldiers farewell," m 4:70,
  73:67
"The soldier's grave," mw 40:3
"Soldiers joy," m 2:32, 5:35,
  13:43, 15:11r, 47:17
"The soldiers last retreat,"
  mw 35:33
"Soldiers march," m 1:25
"Soldier's return," m 52:65
"A solemn dirge in *Romeo and
  Juliet*," mw 9:172
SOLFEGIO EXERCISE, 21:24
"Solitary air," m 1:118, 14:171
"Solo," m 19:118, 19:120-21a
"A solo for the fife," m 14:Er
"Solo for the organ by Mr. Handel,"
  m 18:418
"Some women take delight in dress,"
  mw 4:19
"Somebody," m 52:21; mw 18:298,
  73:55; 21:70 (title only)
Somersworth, N. H., 43
"Something else to do," m 5:76
"Sonata," m 8:27, 8:62, 12:1-2,
  12:27-28, 12:44, 12:54, 18:36,
  18:42-49, 18:54-61, 18:104,
  18:140, 18:164-80, 18:228-48,
  18:258, 18:274, 18:311, 18:424,
  19:4-17, 19:19, 19:26-42,

"Sonata" (*continued*)
  19:50, 19:129, 50:4, 56:1(2),
  56:24, 56:42, 56:58, 83:1, 83:38
"Sonata, sung by a number of young
  girls... Trenton...," m 74
"Sonatas by Eichner," m 10:207
SONATAS: FLUTE AND KEYBOARD,
  56:33; HARPSICHORD, 8:27,
  8:62, 56:1; KEYBOARD, 8:207,
  18:36, 18:42-49, 18:54-61,
  18:103-4, 18:140, 18:164-80,
  18:228-48, 18:258, 18:274,
  18:311, 18:424, 19:4-17, 19:19,
  19:26-42, 19:50, 19:129, 50:4,
  83:1, 83:38, 83:46, 18:56;
  PIANO, 8:27, 12, 56:1; VIOLIN
  AND HARPSICHORD, 56:1; VIOLIN
  AND PIANO, 56:1
"Sonatina," m 56:33, 83:56
"Song," m 50:28, 50:34; mw 9:200-202,
  29, 50:32, 50:35-38, 50:48
"Song by Hook," mw 50:18
"A song for this new militia,"
  mw 84:86
"Song from:" *The deserter*, m 41:19;
  Lodoiska, mw 55:177
"Song in:" *Artaxerxes*, mw 84:24;
  Blue Beard, m 76:83; mw 55:30;
  Comus, mw 9:134; *Eliza*, mw 84:8;
  The fairies, mw 9:156, 9:158; *The
  flitch of bacon*, mw 55:29;
  Harlequins invasion, m 37:33;
  mw 84:12; *Judith*, mw 9:205;
  Lethe, mw 9:168; ___[illegible]
  Lottery, mw 9:160; *The pirates*,
  mw 55:74; *Rosina*, mw 79:35-36;
  Samson, mw 9:188, 9:190, 9:192,
  9:196;*Semele*, mw 9:195; *The
  spoil'd child* m 14:166; *The
  tempest*, mw 9:62
"Song of Diana," mw 9:142
"A song of Major Andrea," m 45:73.
  See also "André's complaint;"
  "Major André's complaint"
SONG-TEXTS, 4:33, 4:61, 4:77,
  4:143-45, 17, 20:4, 21:8, 24,
  31, 41, 44, 47:62-69, 50, 74
"A song to the tune of 'Black
  joke,'" w 74:66
SONGS, 30, 40, 41, 46:57-60, 46:67,
  58:36-39, 74, 77, 80, 85

"Trip it up stairs," m 14:7
"A trip to Halifax," m 20:5
"Trip to Lincoln," m 5:65
"Trip to Nahant," m 80:80
"Trip to Pluckman," m 13:17
"Trip to the little theatre,"
   m 5:64
"Tristram Shandy," m 5:58, 13:73
"The triumph of Bacchus," m 5:152
"The triumph of love," mw 31:18
"Troop," m 2:48, 11:28, 13:106,
   43:15, 47:inside front cover
"Troop for the colours," m 13:106
"The trooper," m 6:48
"The troopers quick step," m 11:27
TROOPS (in titles)
   "Damon & Phyllis," 2:9
   "Doublings of the troop," 2:29
   "Duke of York's," 47:50
   "French," 2:40, 13:26
   "Gramachree," 2:35
   "The grand," 51:48
   "High," 2:38
   "Lord Loudons singling of a," 37:20
   "My troop," 13:17
   "The pilgrim's blith & jolly," 2:31
   "Pools," 13:108
   "The Queen's short," 14:85
   "Short," 81:75
   "Singling of Pools," 13:108
   "The temple," 2:14 [lacking]
Troubadour," mw 15:43*v*
Troy (Asia Minor), 4:86
"The true blue minuet, 1763," m 84:23
"Trumpet air," m 57:6
"Trumpet minuet," m 20:7, 45:68
"Trust in the Lord & his salva-
   tion," mw 83:65
"Truxton forever," m 6:24
"Tu voi ch'io vivao cara,"
   mw 9:8
"Tug Hill," m 47:inside back cover
"Tune in *Apollo and Daphne*,"
   m 47:1
"A tune to Chevy-chase," m 37:47
"The tuneful lavrocks cheer the
   grove," mw 32:30
TUNING, INSTRUCTIONS FOR, 55
"Turkey buzard laugh at crow,"
   m 14:131
"Turkish march," m 27:20

"Turkish music," m 80:76
"Turkish quick step," m 80:79,
   80:158
"The Turks march," m 2:47, 3:30,
   14:113, 32:22
"Turn fair Clora, turn," mw 41:125,
   85:42
"Tutto da voi dipende," mw 7:13
"Twaddle," m 14:51, 14:168
"'Twas [as first word]." *See also*
   "It was"
"'Twas in that season of the year,"
   mw 4:27, 21:57, 41:117
"Twas in the evening of a wintry
   day," mw 50:29
"Twas near a thickets calm retreat,"
   mw 18:302, 32:9
"'Twas on a bank of daisies sweet,"
   mw 53:40
"Twas on a river," mw 57:2 (textual
   incipit only)
"Twas summer and softly the breezes
   were blowing," w 47:62
"'Twas within a mile of Edinburgh,"
   m 14:168; mw 41:38 (textual
   1st line only), 50:1
"Tweed side," m 85:31; mw 9:133,
   41:109
"Twelfth night," mw 41:115
"The 12 days of Christmas," m 37:34
"The 23rd psalm," mw 9:179
"The 25th of November," m 37:21
"Twins of Latona," m 14:141, 32:36;
   mw 41:103, 53:22, 59:2
Two misers, Excerpts, mw 34:57
"Ty Tol," m 45:26

"The unconstant lover," m 37:36
"Under hundert tausend shönen,"
   m 58:12
"Under the blankets," m 5:39
"The unhappy swain," m 13:94, 52:51,
   80:2, 80:140, 82:25
"The union," m 13:72
"The union march," m 18:340
University of Michigan, 29-30
University of Pennsylvania, 67-72
"Unless with Amanda," 7:1 (title only)
"Unless with my Amanda blest,"
   mw 7:2

"Yo-yea," m 14:157, 47:61
"Yomam a knuck," m 14:179
"York Battalions quick march."
    See "Second York Battalions
    quick march"
York, Duke of, 1:52, 1:72, 3:29,
    4:122, 13:110, 14:115, 17:47,
    18:330, 47:48, 47:50, 48:36,
    52:63, 55:22, 58:24
York, Dutchess of, 14:64
"York fusiliers," m 6:12, 11:34,
    13:54, 14:60, 21:77, 45:47,
    80:32
"York fuzeleers duet," m 1:95,
    17:17
"York shire," m 13:72
"Yorkshire lads," m 37:19
"You be welcome here again,"
    m 13:74
"You gentlemen of England that
    live at home at ease," mw 21:53
"You may if you will," m 14:58
"You may say that," m 14:10
"You spotted snakes with double
    tongue," mw 9:156
"You the point," m 11:29
"Young Collin protests," mw 9:90

"Young Damon has woode me a monstrous
    long time," mw 73:56
"The young farmer," m 37:39
"The young girl," m 37:45
"Young Henry was as brave a youth,"
    mw 58:62
"Young Jack," m 2:16
"Young Jockey is the lid for me,"
    m 14:165
"Young Johnny the miller,"
    mw 4:61
"Young Strephon a shepheard, the
    pride of the plain," mw 9:154
"Young Strephon a shepherd,"
    m 5:70, 47:33
"The young widow," m 6:62, 13:40,
    14:10, 52:57, 80:6
"Your bobbin' the black," mw 73:31
"Your care of money, ah care naw
    more," mw 35:56
"A youth adorn'd," mw 9:126

"The zephyr," m 80:79
"Zura," mw 80:39